AF573992

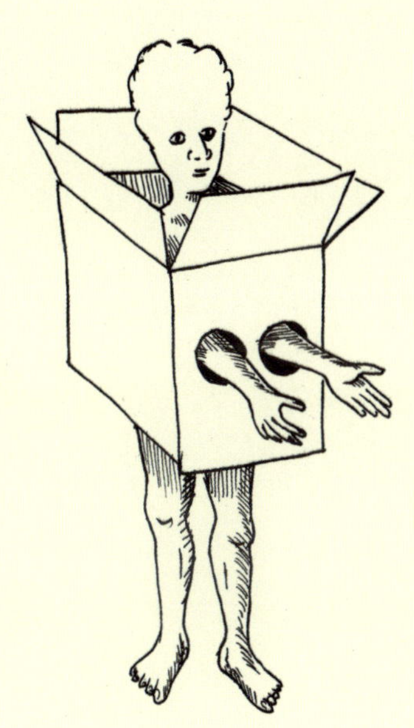

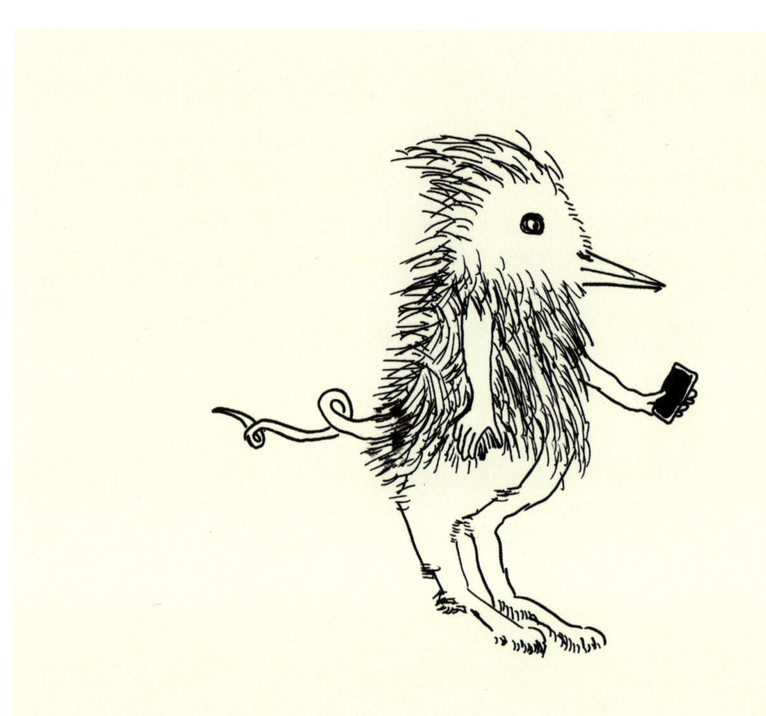

A HISTORY *of* THE WORLD

(*in* DINGBATS)

DRAWINGS & WORDS
DAVID BYRNE

DIRECTION & DESIGN
ALEX KALMAN

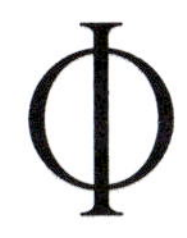

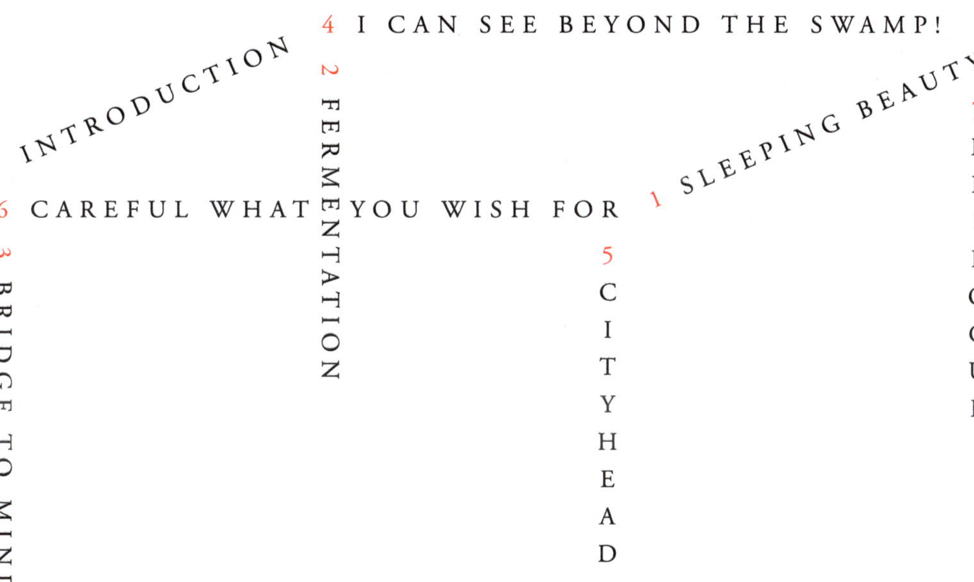
INTRODUCTION
1 SLEEPING BEAUTY
2 FERMENTATION
3 BRIDGE TO MIND
4 I CAN SEE BEYOND THE SWAMP!
5 CITYHEAD
6 CAREFUL WHAT YOU WISH FOR
7 EPILOGUE

INTRODUCTION

A STORY MADE OF PICTURES

Dingbats?
Isn't a dingbat a stupid person? Yes, that's the common usage.

But that meaning may have derived from the word for a meaningless typographical element—nonsense symbols used by typesetters long ago both to give layout instructions to a printer (a person, not a machine) and to create visual breathing space in a type layout.

These meaningless glyphs eventually morphed into little drawings and icons that are often used to break up imposing and intimidating blocks of text. A flowerpot, a bird, a cup and saucer, that kind of thing—they're not usually meant to illustrate specific text content.

My drawings were conceived in that tradition, as a library of drawings to be used by the editors of the *Reasons To Be Cheerful* web magazine, but as soon as I began to draw I got carried away . . . they immediately assumed a life of their own. The editors didn't seem to mind, and, once open, the faucet flowed.

The drawings in this book were all made during the time of Covid . . .
and quite often I can sense that mood comes through.
I can see there are thoughts about one's body,
one's mental state,
one's priorities and values,
one's household routines,
the world beyond one's house or apartment.

Has my physical body, in effect, confined me?
Did I forget to dump the kitchen compost?
Am I wondering if we're all descending into apartment squalor?
Or is it just me?
Do I need to shower for a Zoom call?
Do I have to wear long pants?

What really matters to me?
Have we all been going along in our lives
without stopping to question anything?
Aren't other people what really matter to me?

Although I didn't realize it when I began, the drawings fell into recurring categories. These became the chapters, and in a way they accumulate, as our experiences did, and a kind of narrative emerges.

My own fears and desires—
which I assume are shared by so many others
who have gone through and survived
this surreal, tragic, revelatory, and unsettling experience—
are not unique.

We who have survived have been transformed—in ways we are often unaware of.
These changes in who we are and how we feel keep mutating and changing.
How we felt when this began is not how we felt a year later—
that seems pretty obvious.

These drawings, I realize, have become a record, a history, of those changes.

My hope is that others will recognize themselves in some of these images.
I assume that, like songs, they're not just about me.

Does everyone remember the days when touch transmission was a worry?
(It turned out to be very unlikely.)
When every door handle or railing was a thing to be avoided?

It seems to me we can't wait to move on—no surprise—but there is the risk of forgetting. The curtain was pulled back on "normal" and it became obvious that we actually didn't want things to go back exactly as they were.
It is a moment to imagine how things can be better than that.

The drawings are not a direct commentary on specific societal issues laid bare—but maybe they begin to articulate how we feel. Joyous yet also frozen.
Fragmented yet unified.

Those feelings will stay with us for a long time,
when specifics are long forgotten.
They become part of who we are.

The titles of the drawings are, I believe, often integral to what they are. While calling an artwork "untitled" does generously open it up to wider interpretation, it also shows a lack of commitment. Give your child a name!

I often look at one of these drawings, just before I title it, and I ask myself, "But what is it *really* about?" The titles are sometimes an attempt to answer that question, or at least they hint at a meaning beyond a simple literal interpretation.

It's hard to put it into words, but if a friend chuckles while looking at some of these then I presume they understand that sometimes a drawing of cheese is not just a drawing of a fermented dairy product. Their reaction makes me smile because I sense they too realize it's really about something else. It's maybe something we've all been experiencing, and this is a way of sharing and recognizing that.

The history of the world is a story we tell ourselves.

Though the permanency of writing has slowed the process, these stories we tell ourselves about the world are not fixed. They are ever and continually revised and changed. History is not what happened, but it is what we agree happened—shaped by our biases and self-serving interests.

Stories are lessons we send to ourselves—some remain vibrant and relevant while others are only useful for a moment. They serve myriad purposes that are often beyond our ken, for better or worse, and sometimes both at the same time.

Propaganda and parables,
delight and deception,
mystery and manipulation.

Here is a story of a time
made of pictures with names.

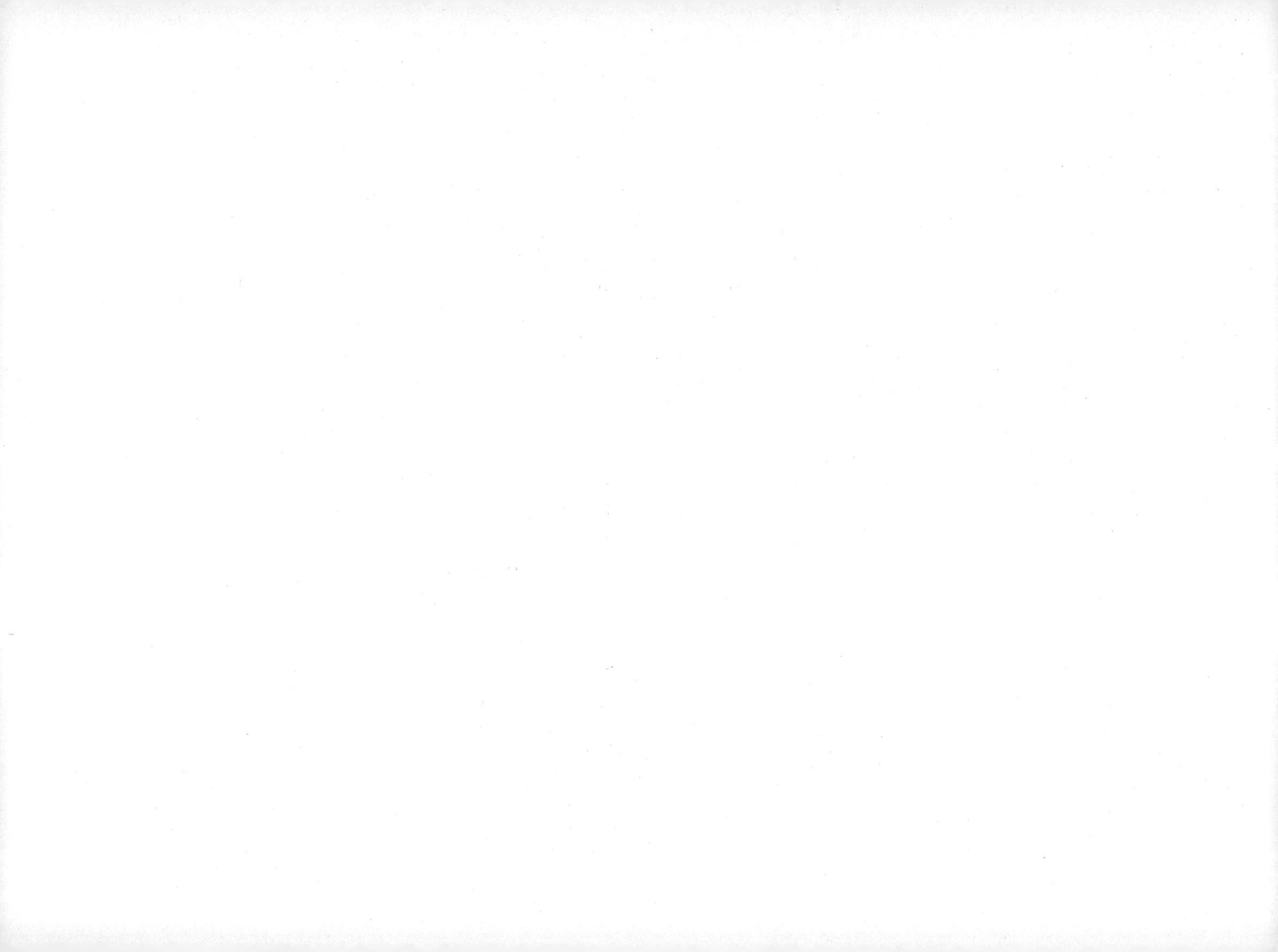

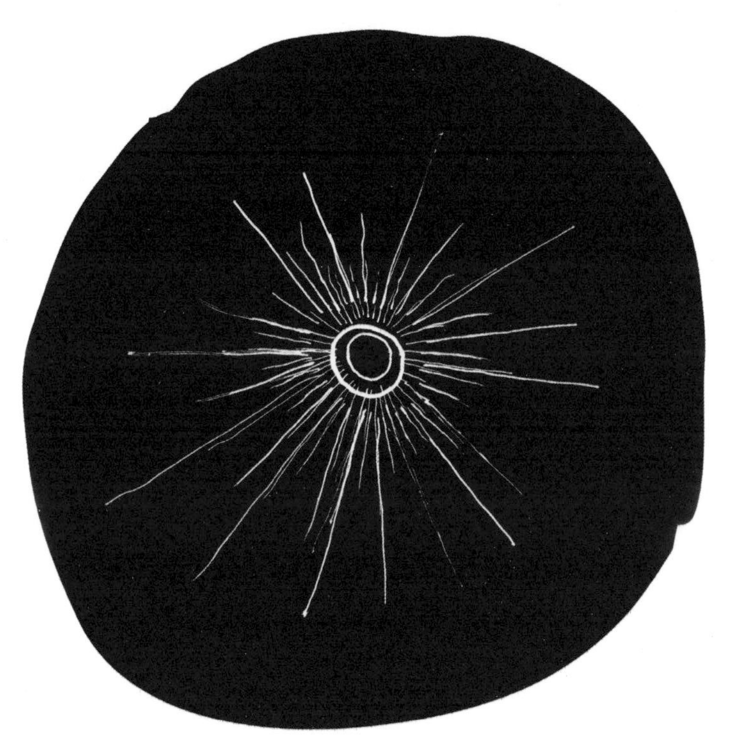

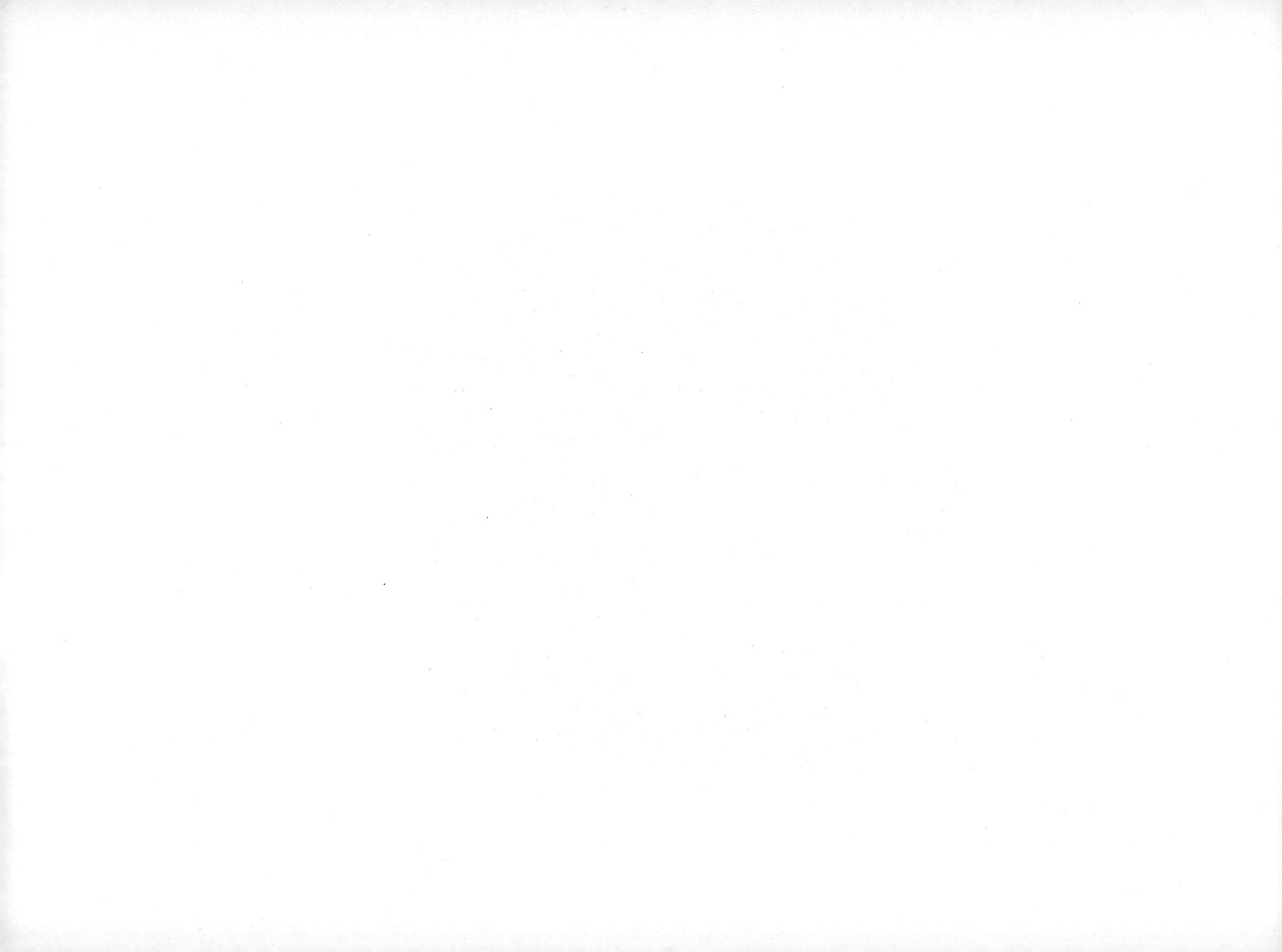

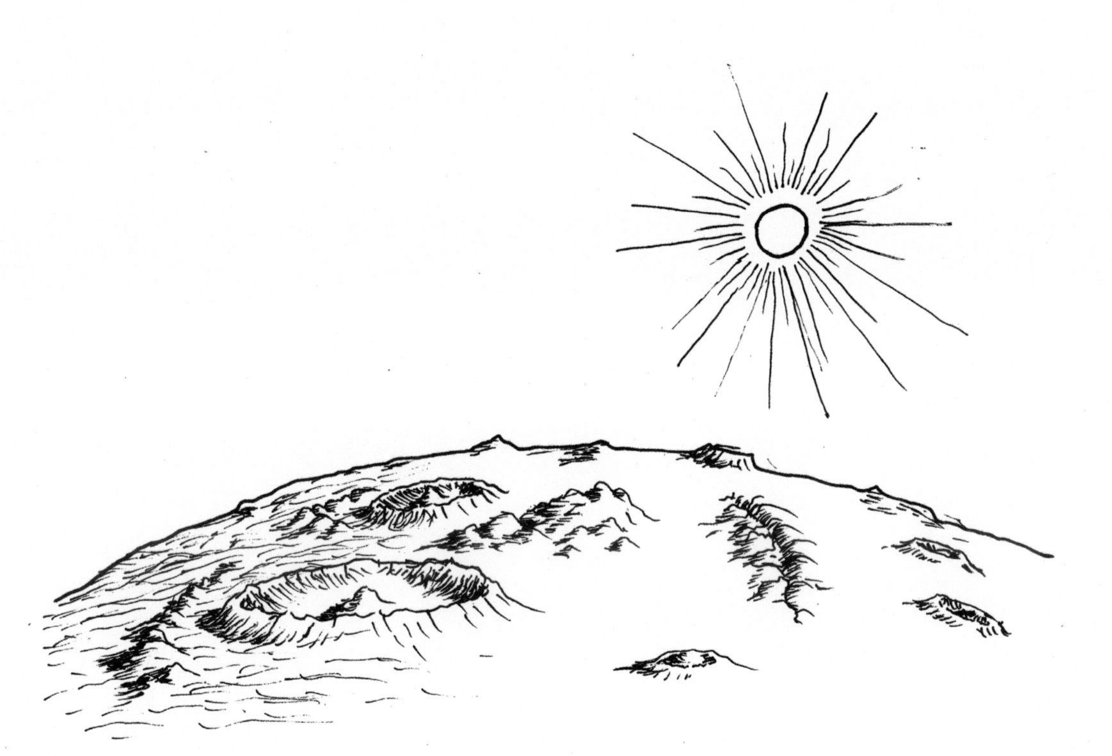

PART ONE

SLEEPING BEAUTY

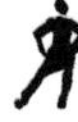

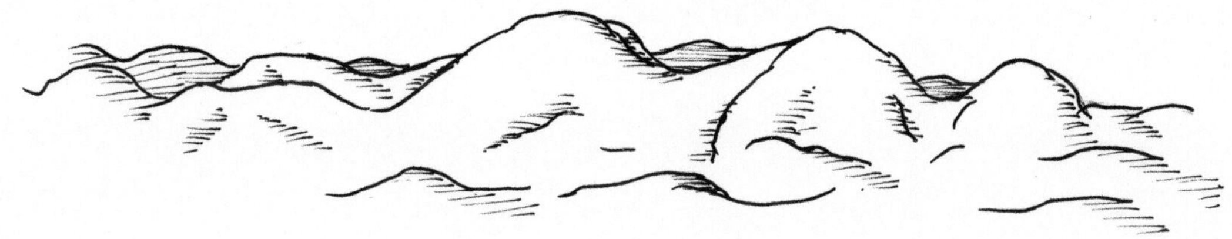

Throughout history, some ideas, connections, perspectives, and technologies have emerged, come into view, and then often go to sleep. Brilliant inventions, stories, and techniques can vanish from our view, sometimes for long periods, lying dormant until someone wakes them.

About 2,400 years ago Democritus proposed that everything is made of atoms. That they can't be destroyed and that sweet things are made of round atoms and that bitter things are made of sharp, spiky atoms. Aristotle—brilliant, influential, and wrong—said no, there weren't lots of atoms, just four elements.

The idea of atoms was put to sleep. Aristotle's influence was so profound, this deep and peaceful slumber lasted about 2,000 years until the idea was awakened in England by John Dalton in 1808. He too claimed that each element was made of identical atoms that cannot be destroyed. The sweet and bitter theory might be beautiful poetry, but it's not true. But 2,000 years! And we take this idea for granted now!

The list of sleepers is long. Like mountains and oceans, dark forests and remote landscapes, they surround us, interred, peaceful, and unrecognized. Concrete, steam engines, clocks—all created and forgotten. Not just technological innovations and scientific insights but also artists, writers, and their works are often forgotten too. Bruegel, Caravaggio, Melville, Fernando Pessoa—all were consigned to oblivion or misplaced for decades or even centuries.

Surely even now many more lie slumbering among and around us. Some of them are known unknowns, like the missing works of Aristotle or Shakespeare—we know of their existence, but they are lost. Others are the unknown unknowns—works and insights so invisible to us that we have forgotten they ever existed.

Beautiful insights, marvels, and miracles lie everywhere, peacefully awaiting a gentle touch or recognition. As we emerge into a new world we may be able to finally remove our veils and see them all around us.

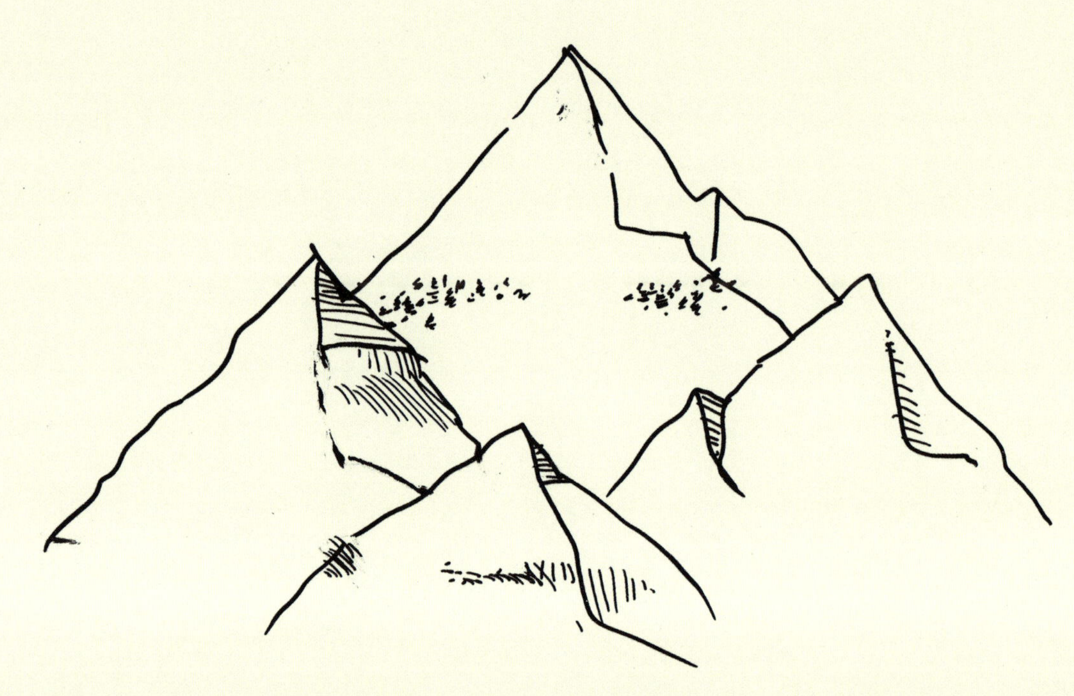

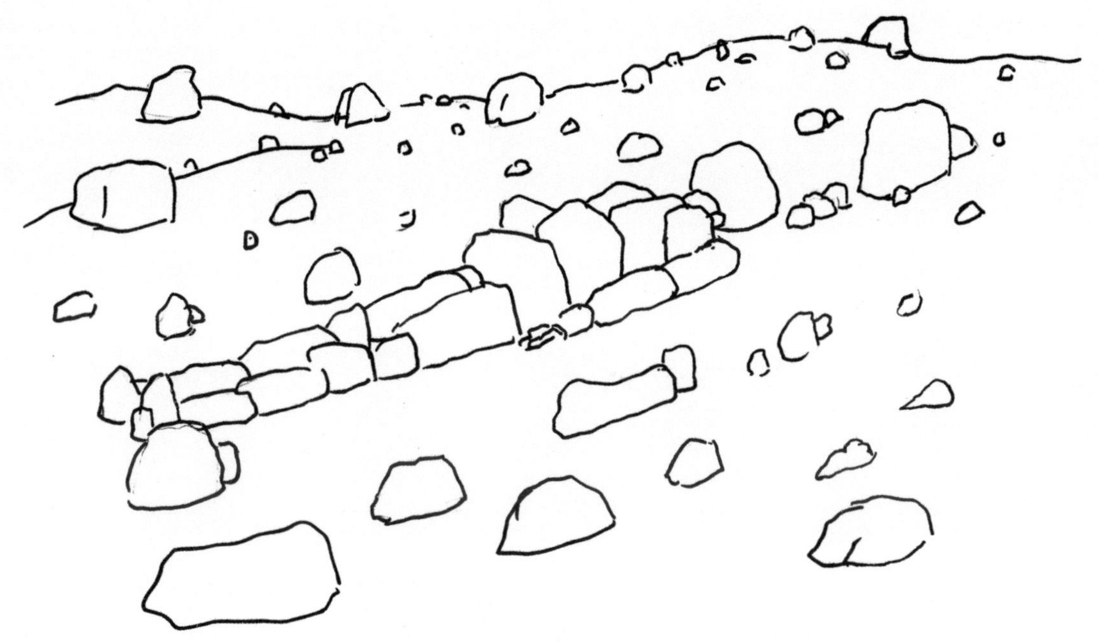

CHTHONIC

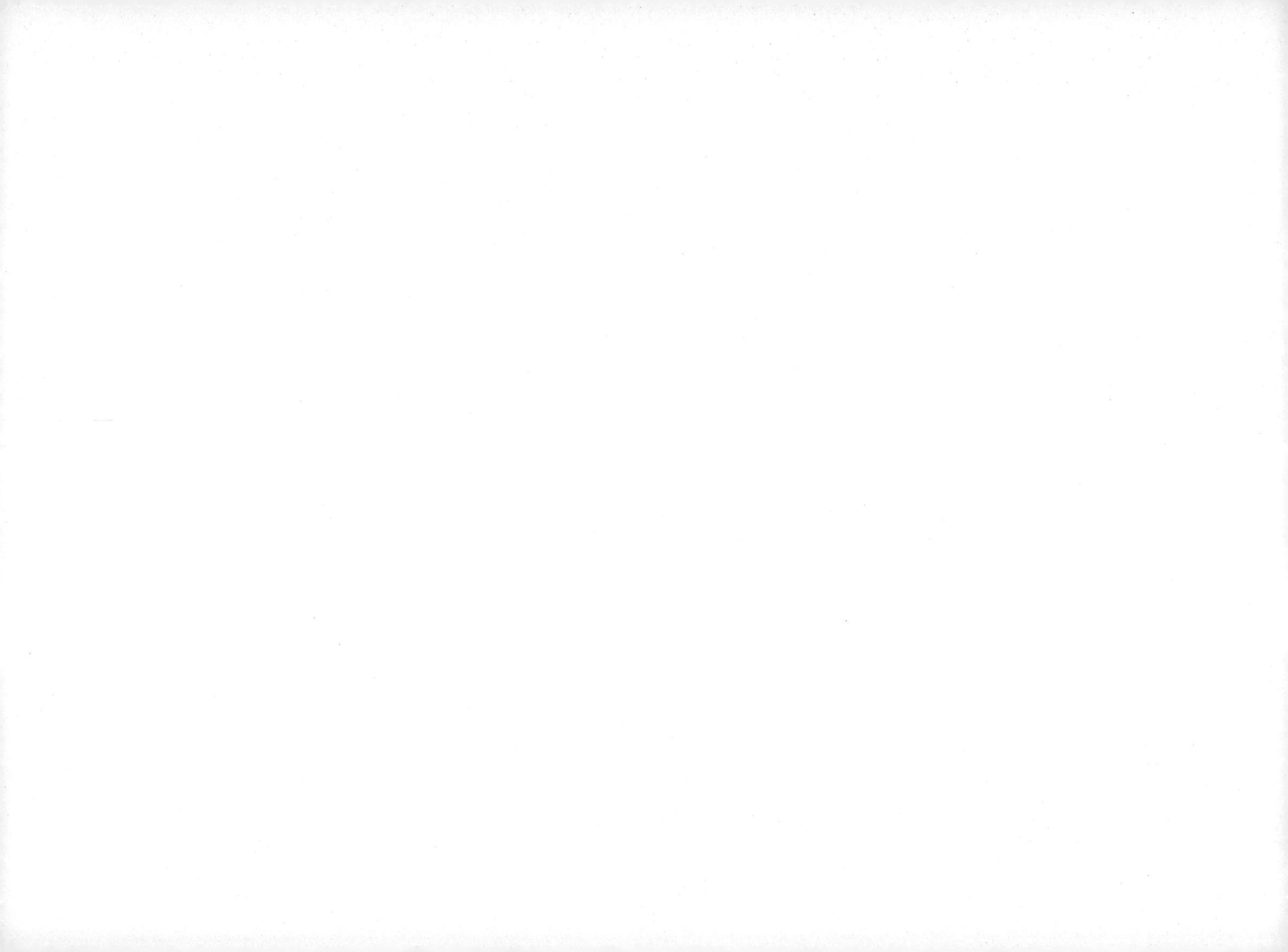

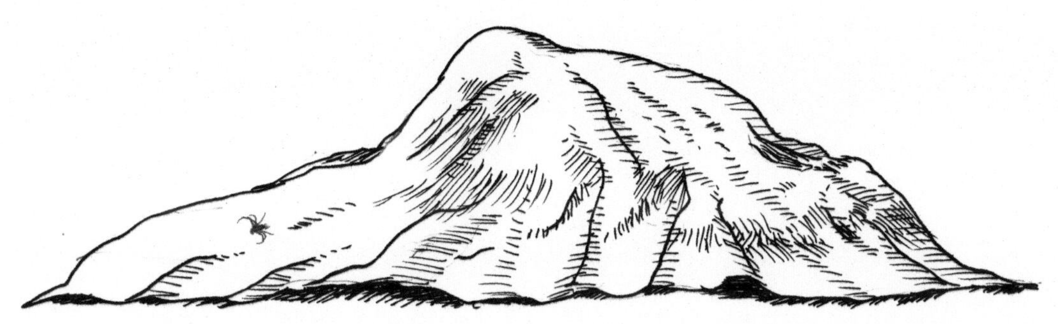

UNCOVERED

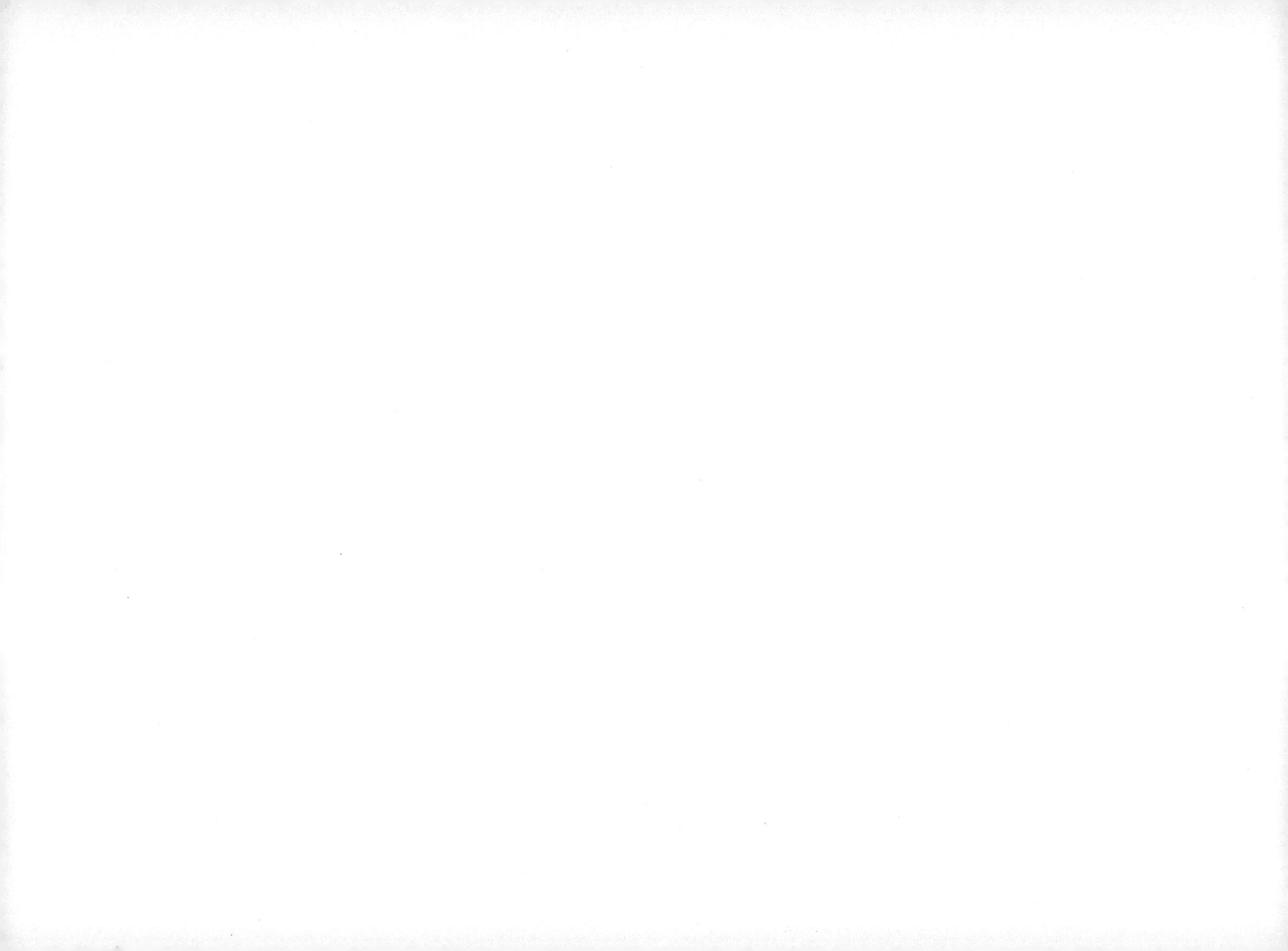

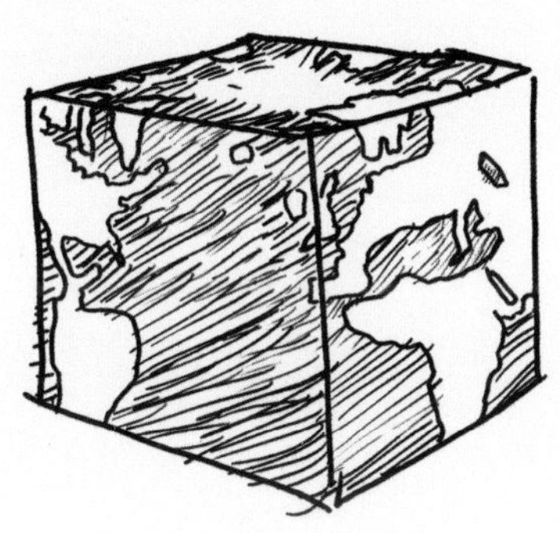

THE REASONABLE WORLD

PART TWO

FERMENTATION

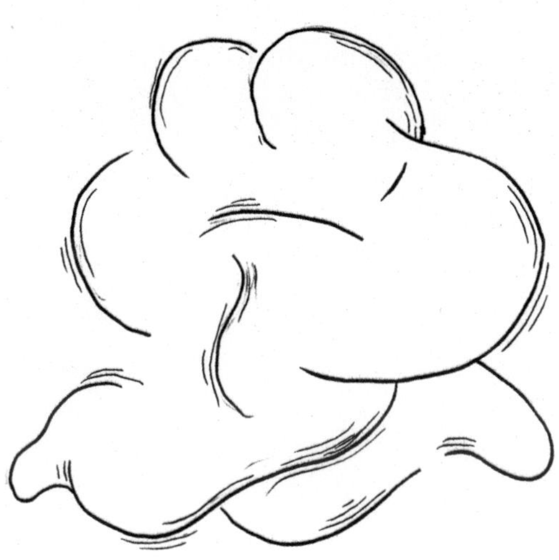

A process in organic matter that produces chemical changes and the extraction of energy.

Often recognized at the microbial level, it also takes place on a macro level as a kind of coming together,
conjunction,
and collaboration,
resulting in merging
and transformation.

It can both preserve and destroy.
We cannot live without it though too much is fatal.

It is the same in the realm of thought and feeling—
emotional fizziness and intellectual disruption.
Drunk on love and bubbling new insights.

We are not a brain in a box, separate from our bodies,
our senses, and the billions of microbes that live within us.

Love, sex, desire, hunger, and the need to be together
may make us less than rational.

We may live in a world of our own imagining,
but it allows us to dance, sing, and do a thousand things
that machines may never be able to do without programming.

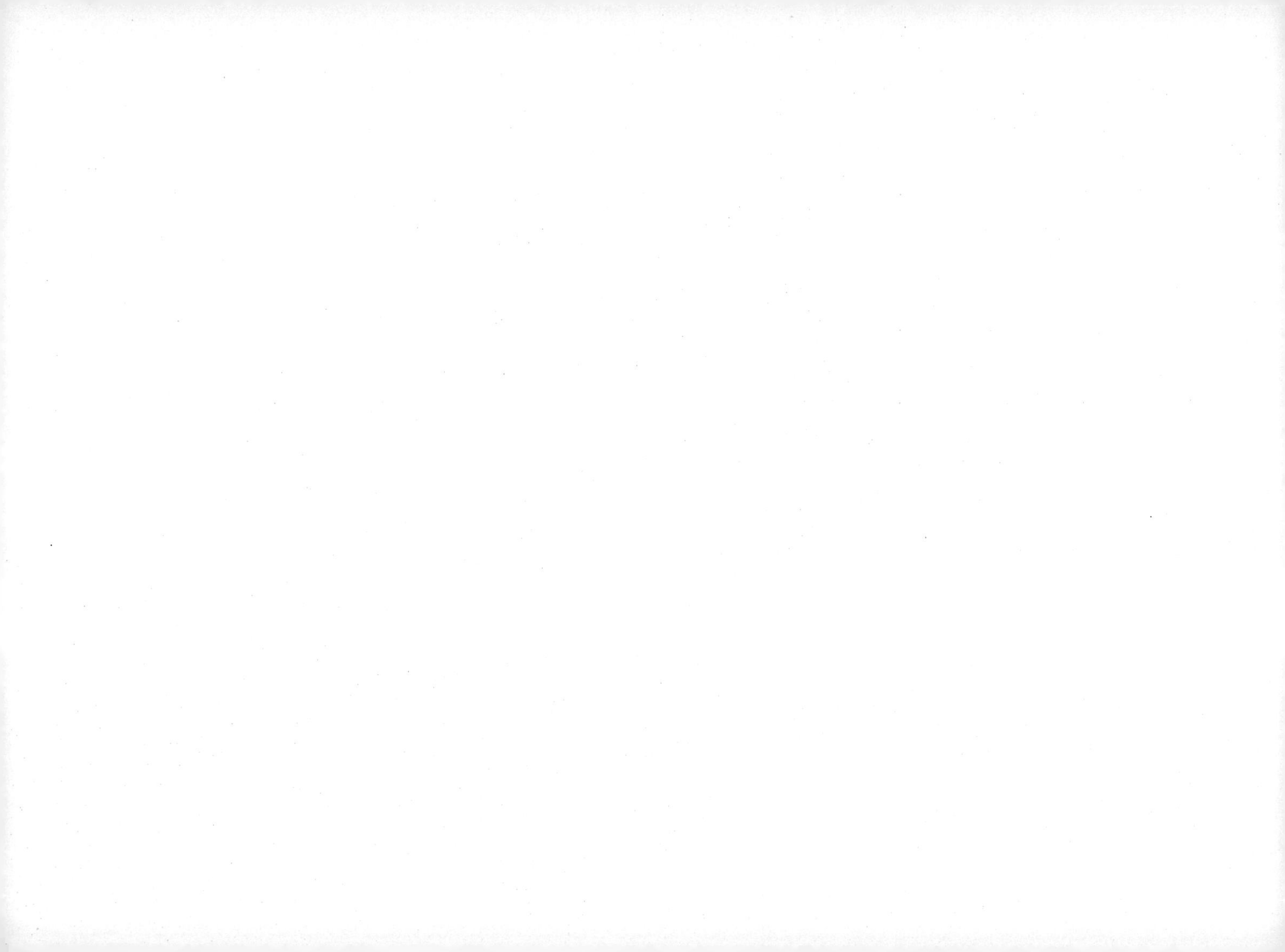

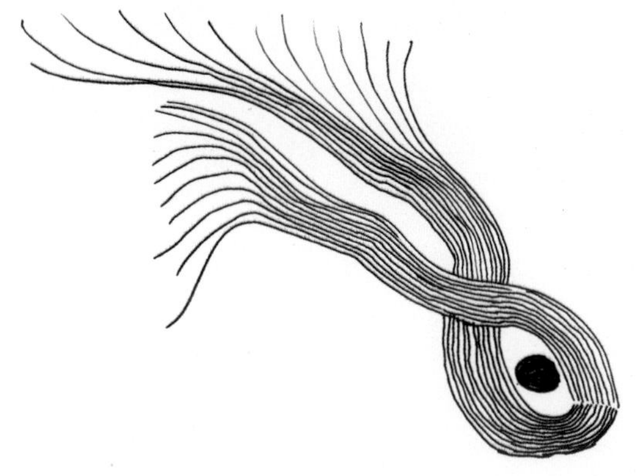

PORTRAIT

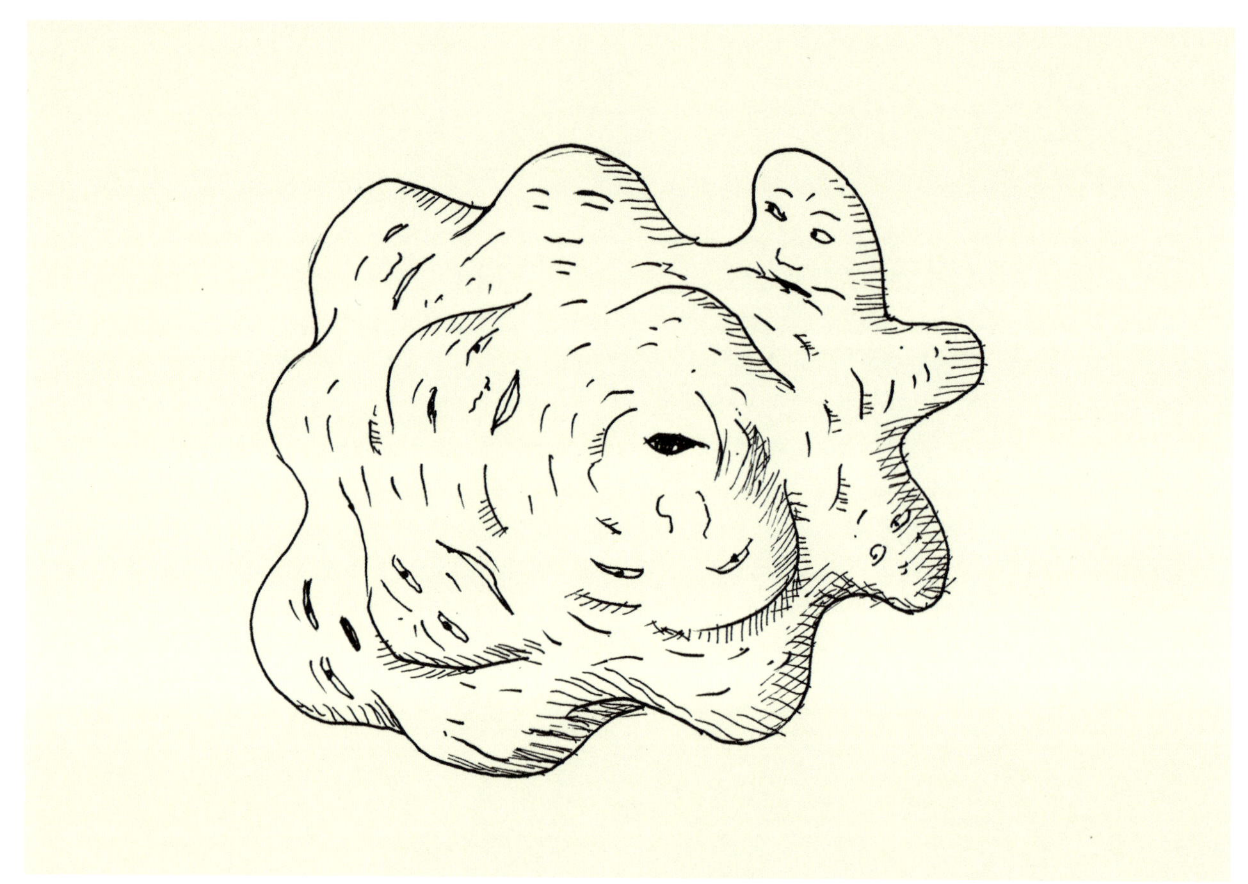

CELLULAR AWARENESS

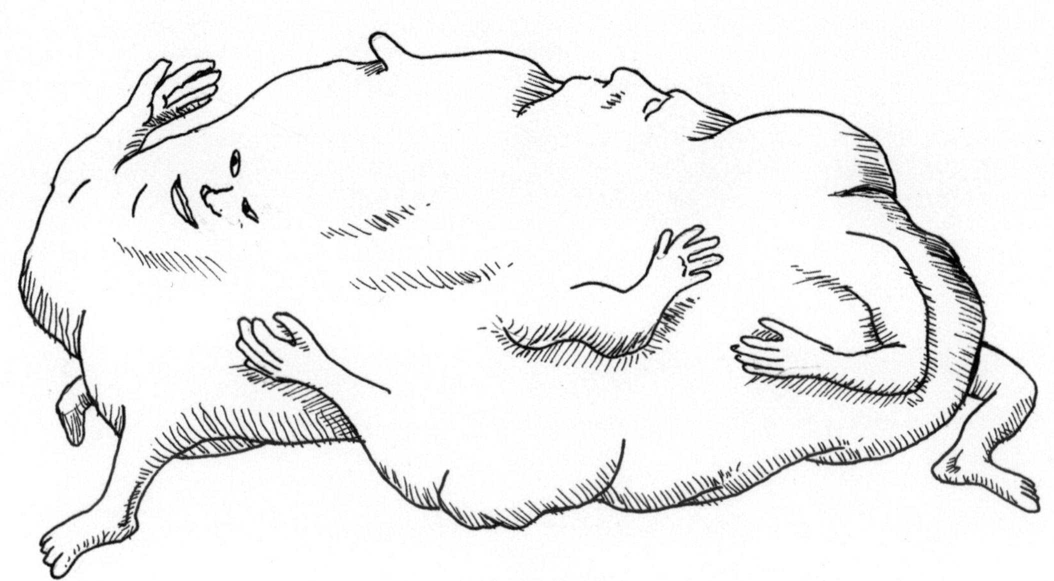

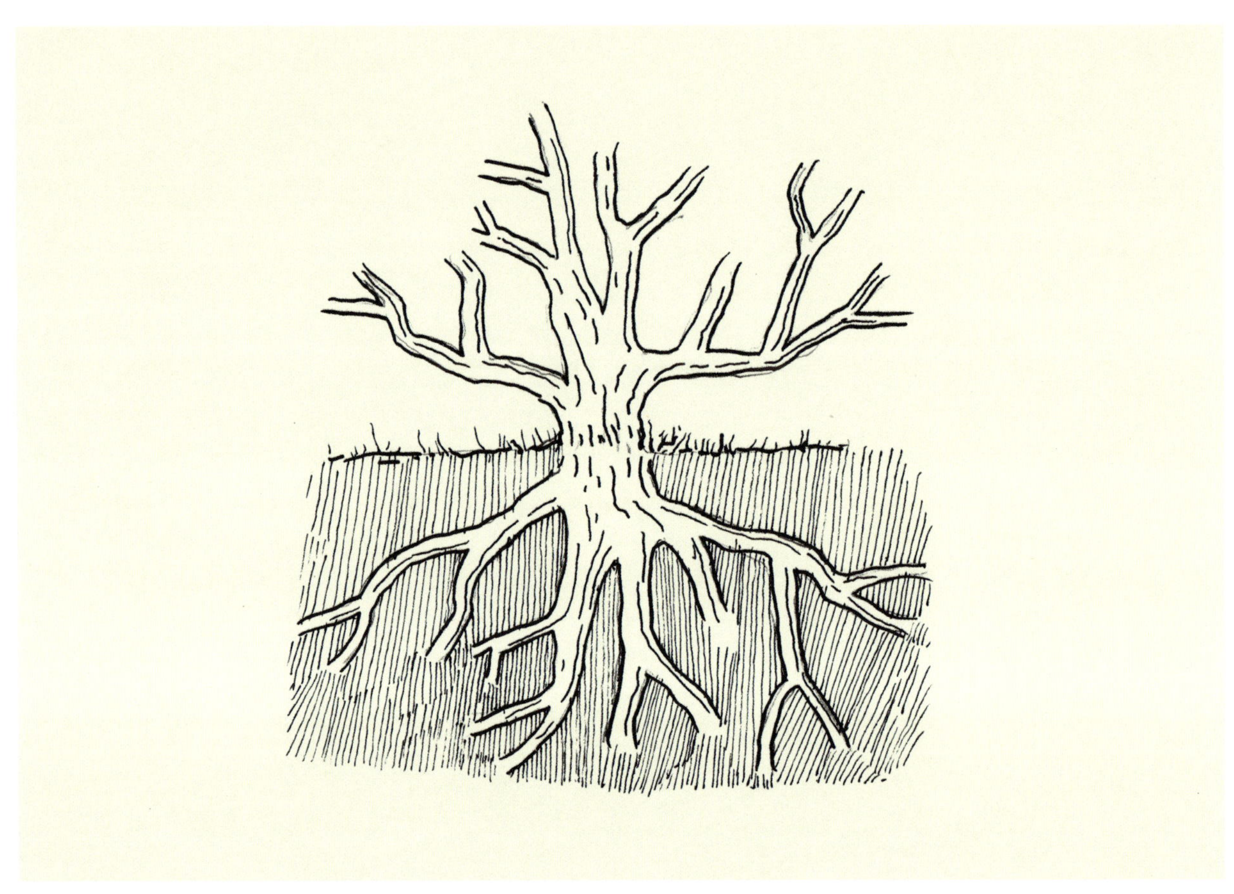

AS ABOVE SO BELOW

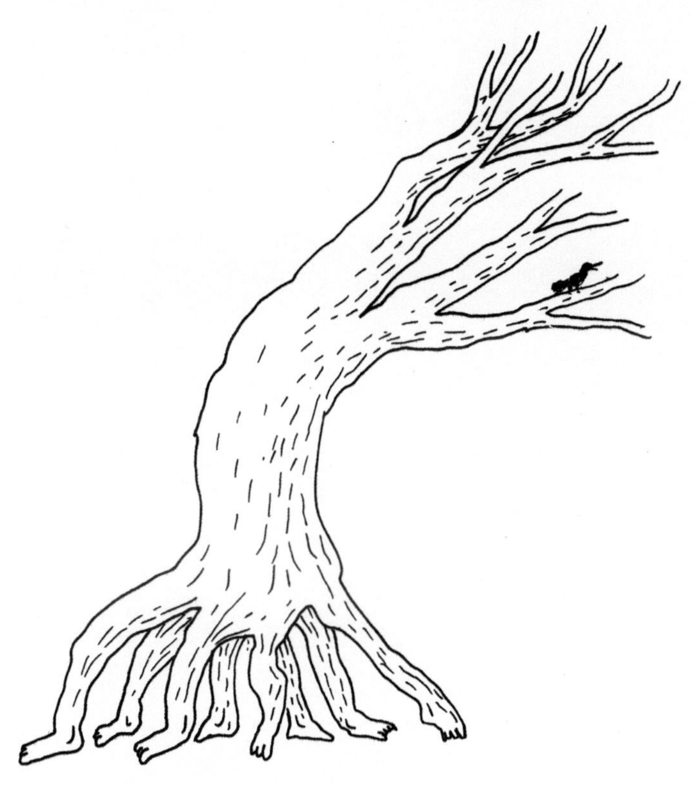

ARBOREAL MIGRATION

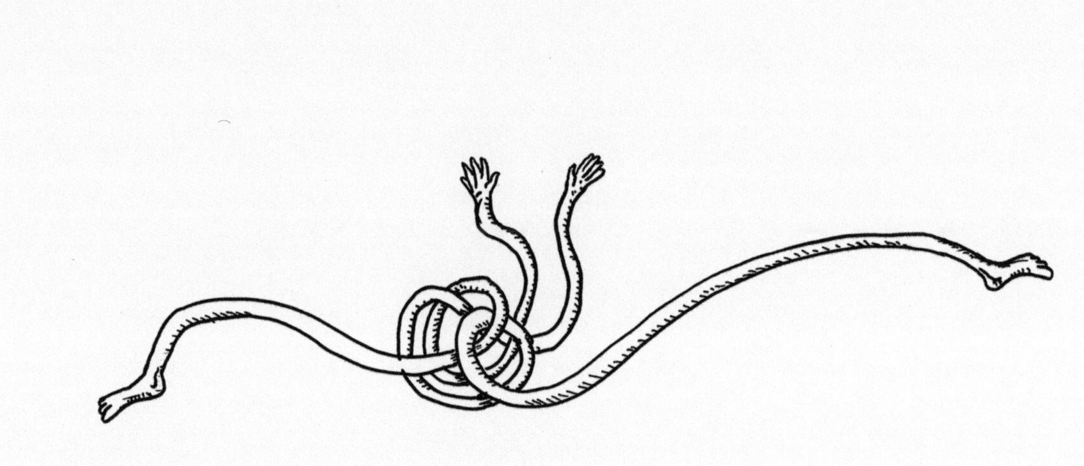

REACH

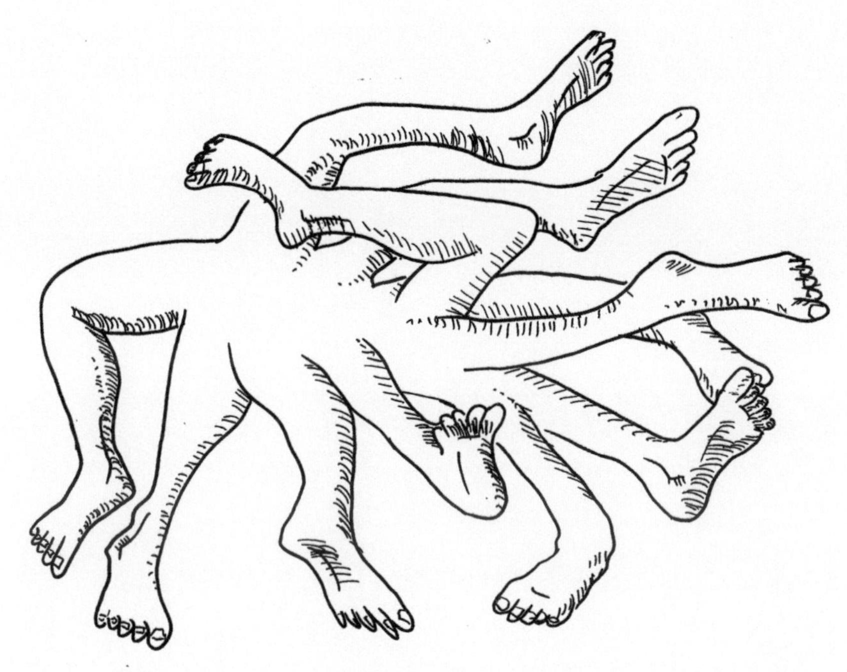

BEST FOOT FORWARD

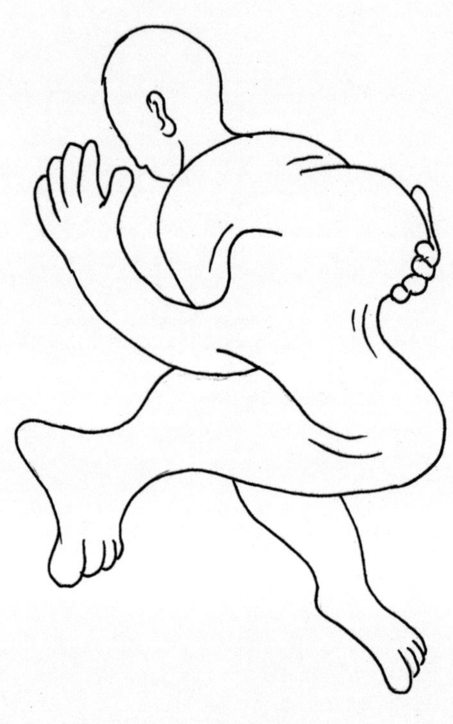

PROPRIOCEPTION

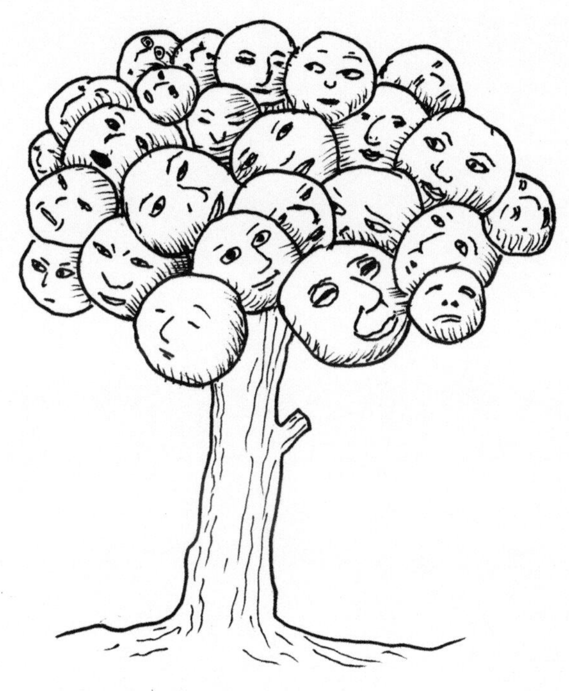

FAMILY TREE

PART THREE

BRIDGE TO MIND

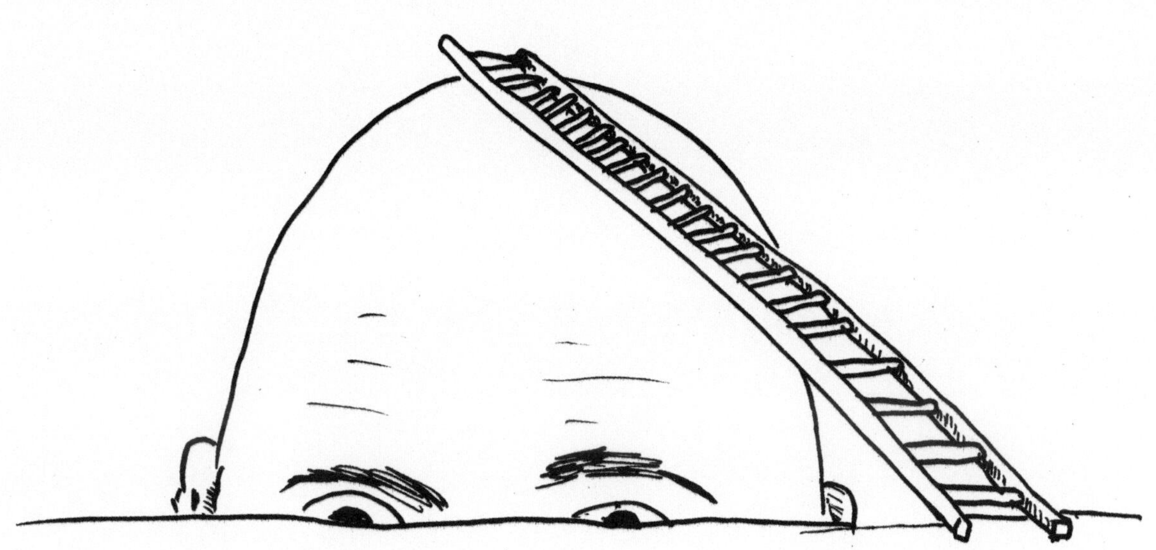

Rolled up in tissue paper.
Secured with a rubber band.
Rooms where we dwell.
Thoughts and feelings accumulate,
like unread books and junk mail.

There, almost hidden under a pile of cleaning solutions and electronic chargers,
is a paper window to the life I used to know.

This is you, it says.
But it's not me *now*.

Who was I then? Would I like myself, even?
Would the person I'm with like me?
Is there forward momentum,
  as it seems to feel to us,
    or are we moving sideways?

   What's going on in there?
Are there other people in there with me?
      Are you there too, my love?

Every book I've read,
every street, face, and song.
I'm made of people and things outside myself,
beyond myself, and beyond my own control.
                    Here is the miracle.

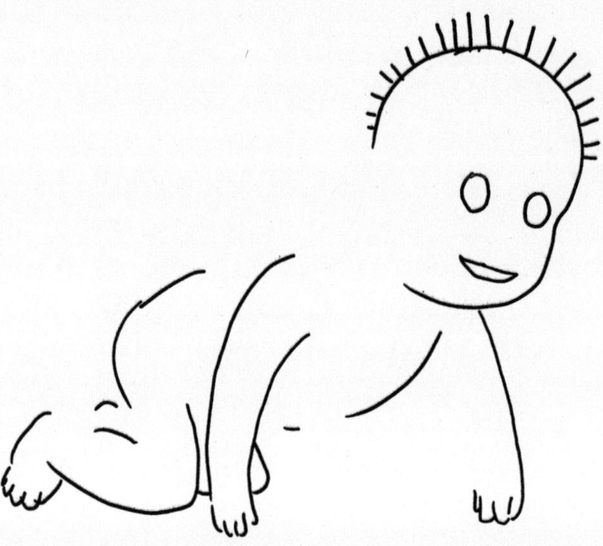

THE CURIOUS BABY

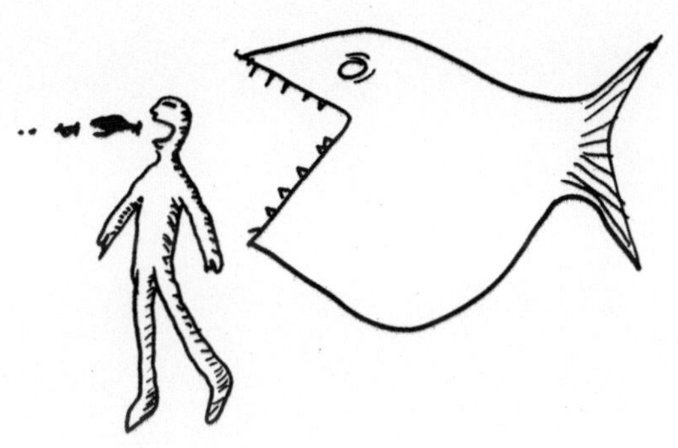

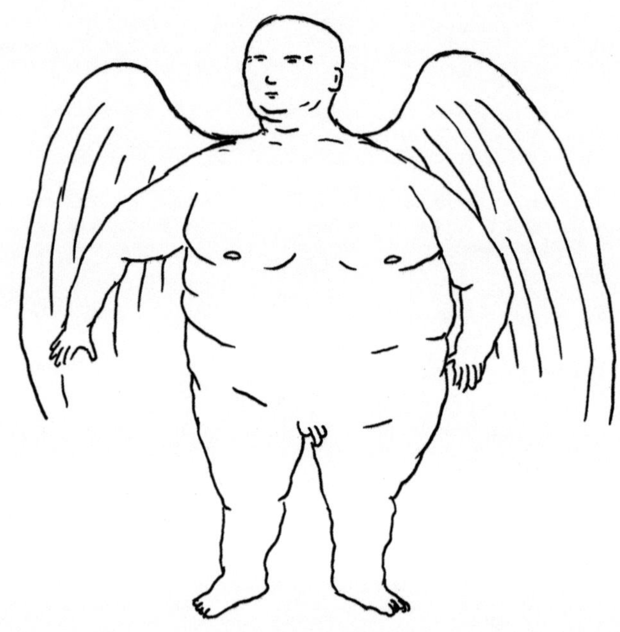

PUTTO GROWN UP

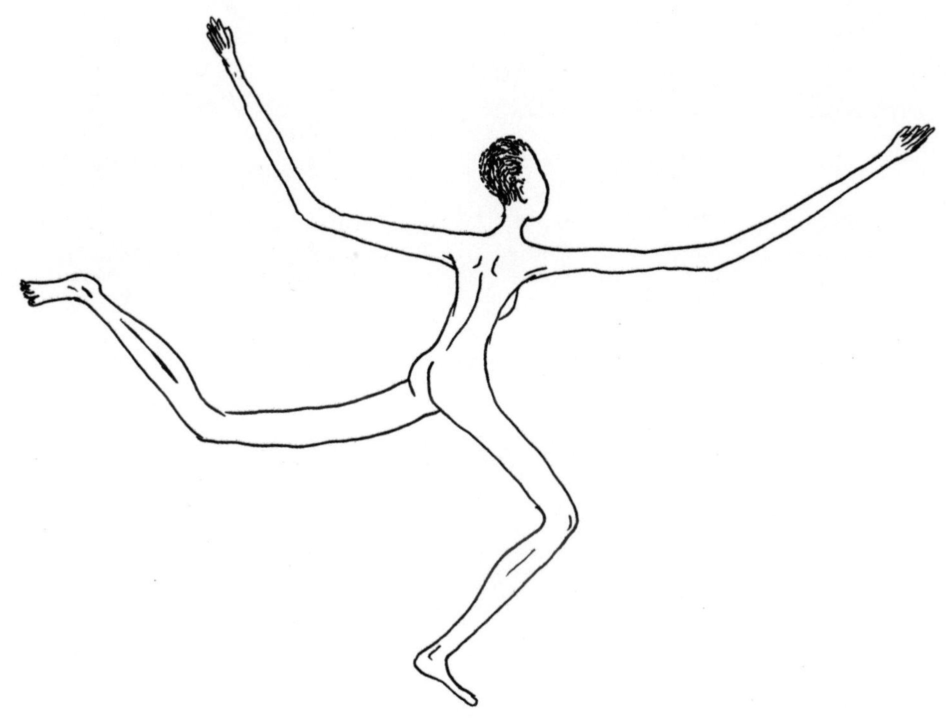

BOUNDING

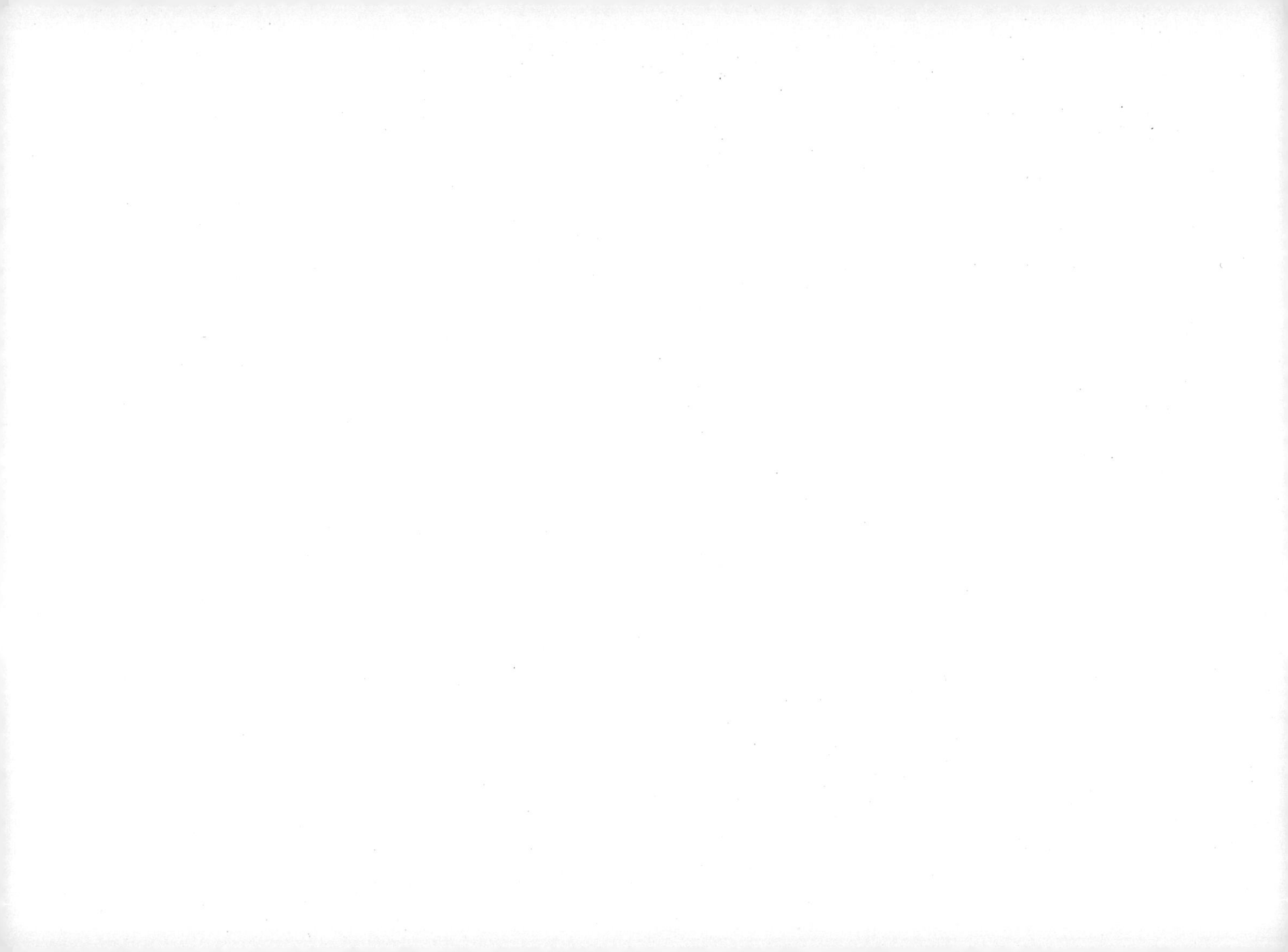

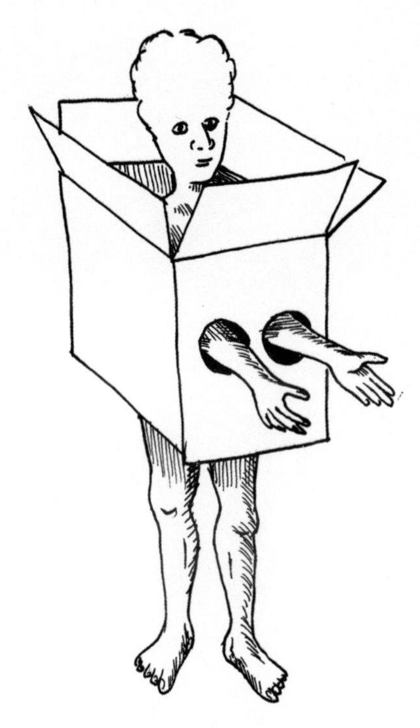

BOX GAME

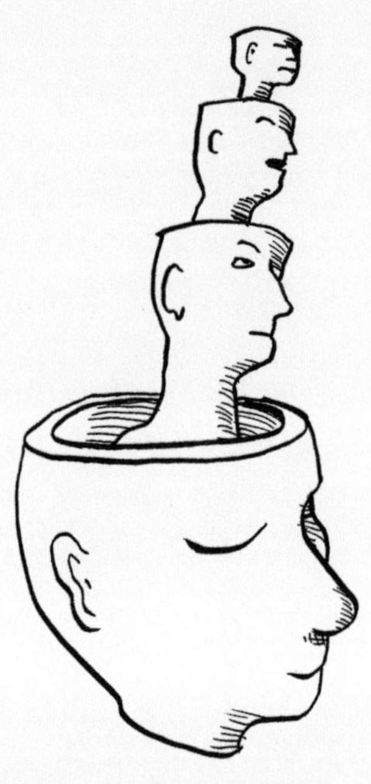

THOUGHTS INSIDE OF THOUGHTS

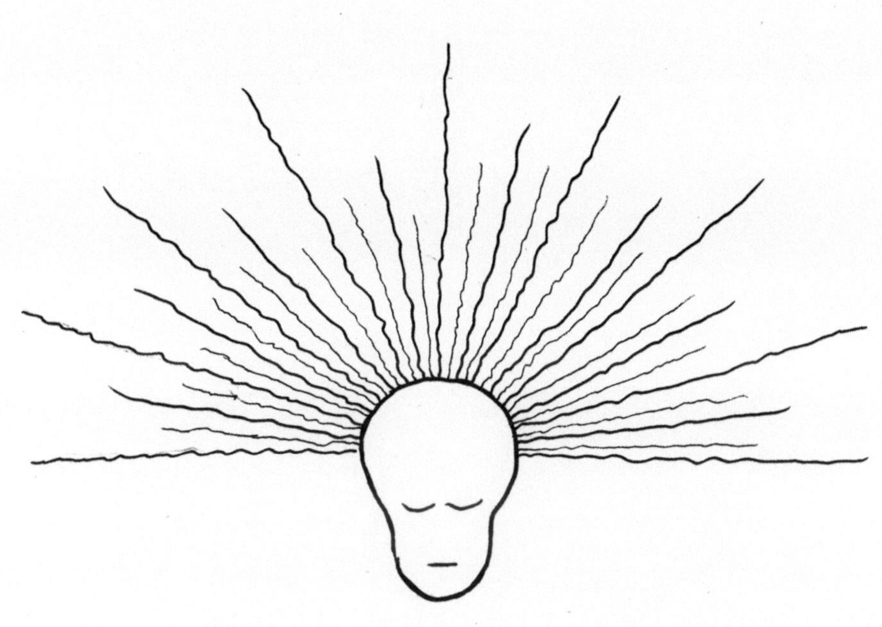

INTROSPECTION

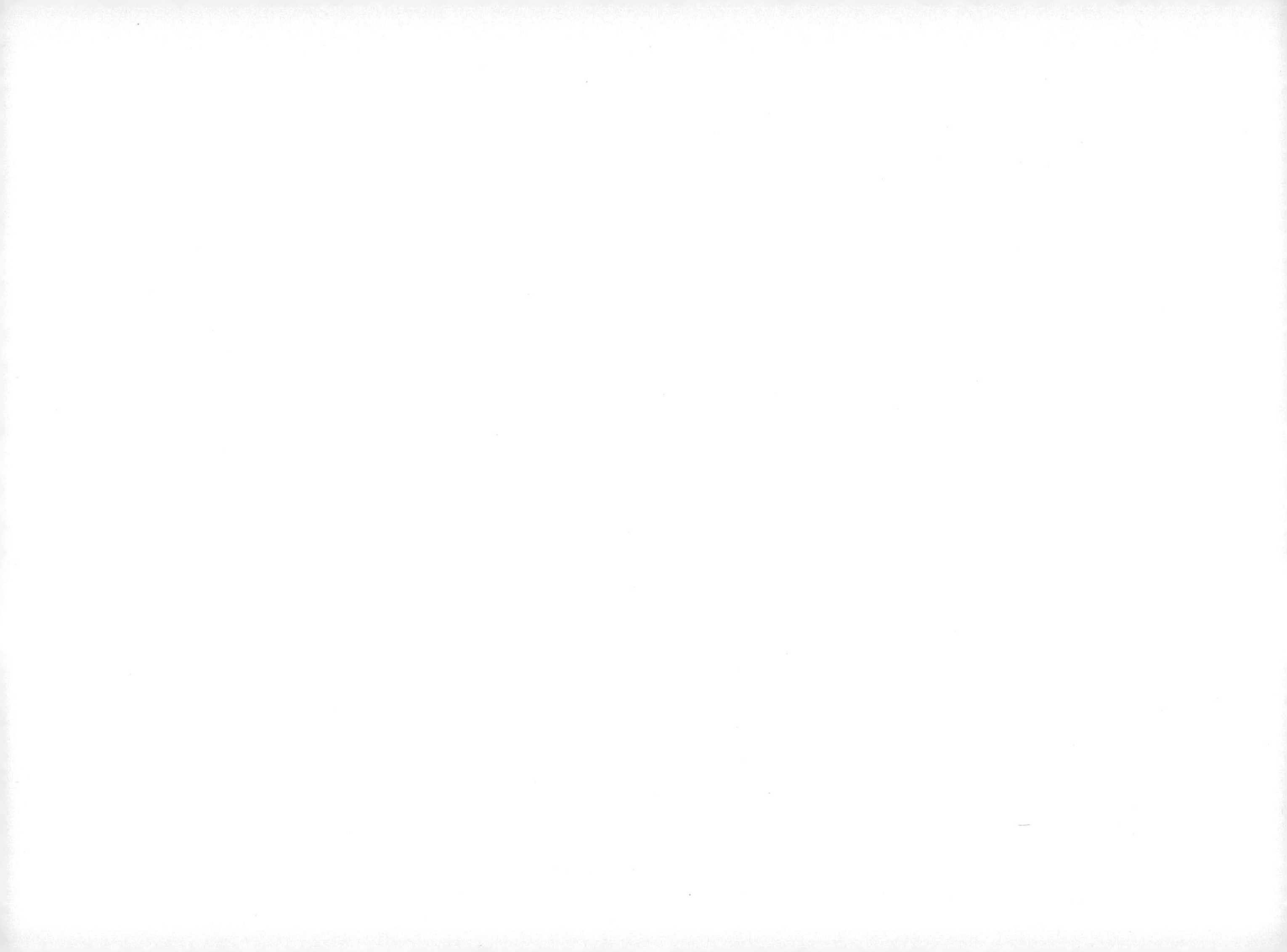

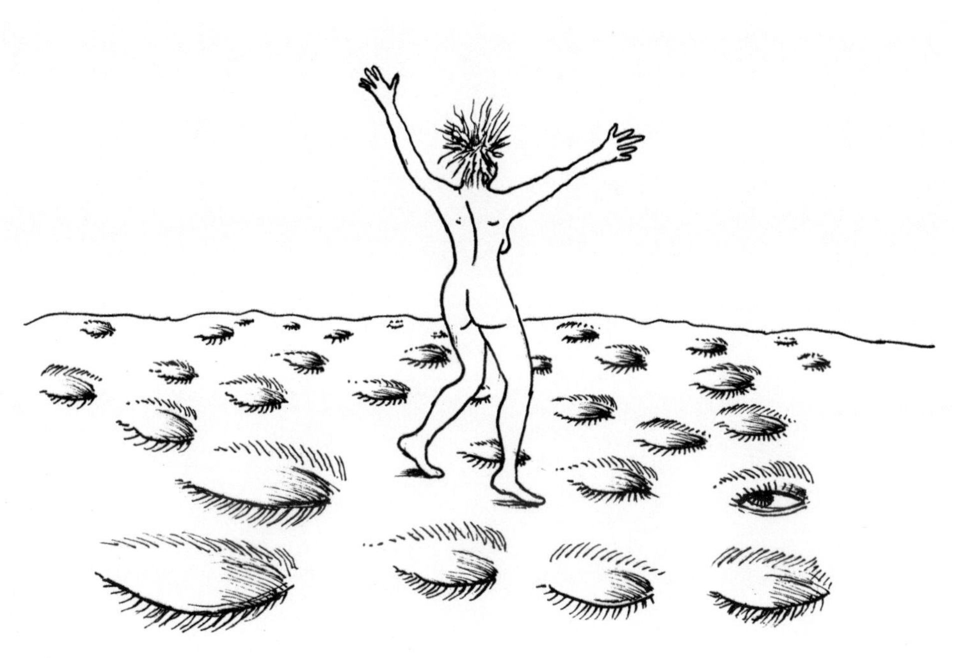

INTELLECTUAL MINEFIELD

READ ME

DRINK ME

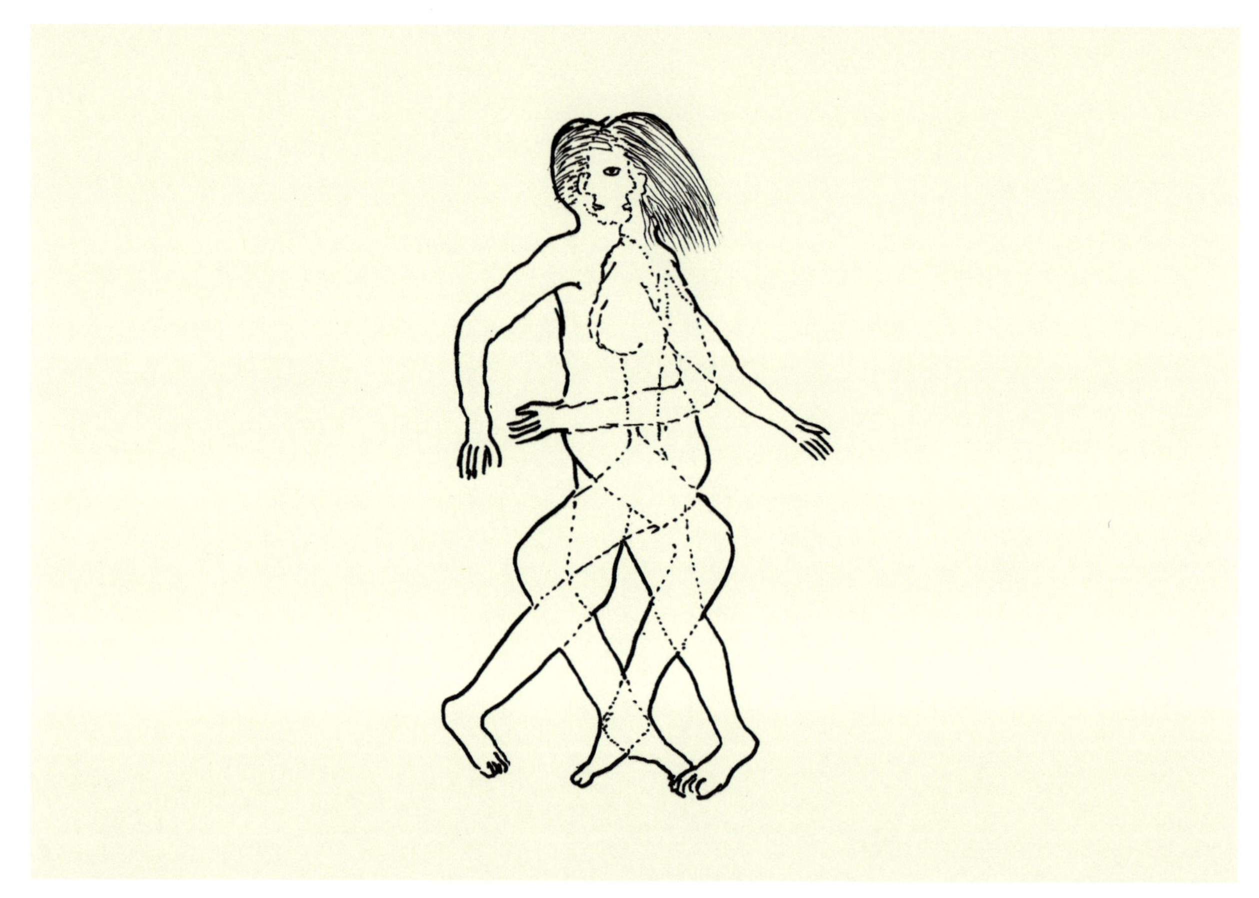

SEEING THROUGH YOU

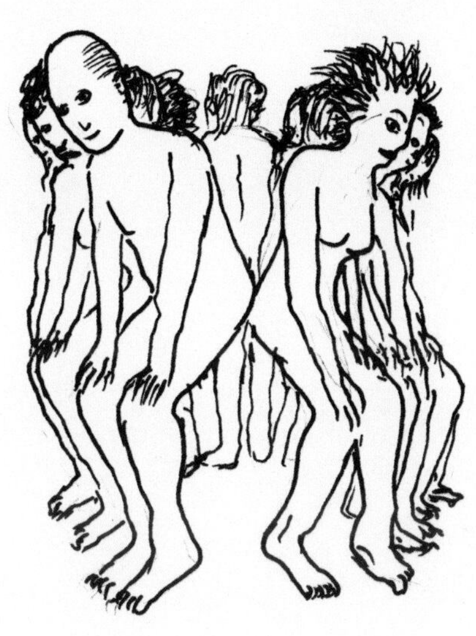

BUTT'IN IN — CHEEK TO CHEEK

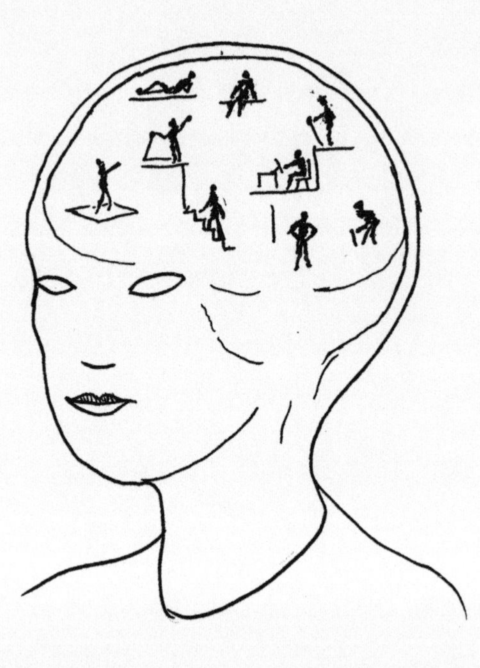

UNDERSTANDING HER IS EASY

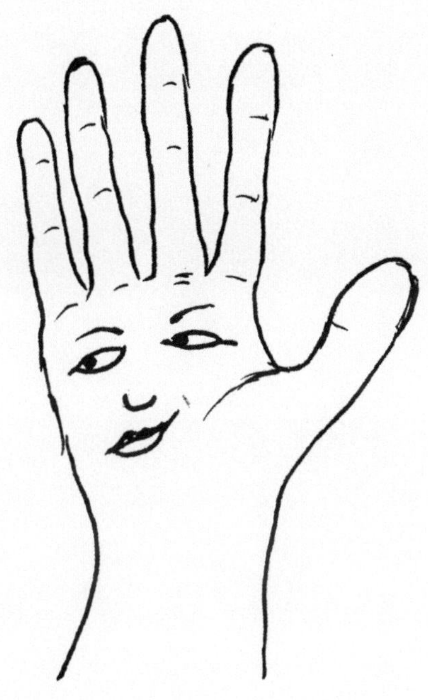

TALK TO THE HAND

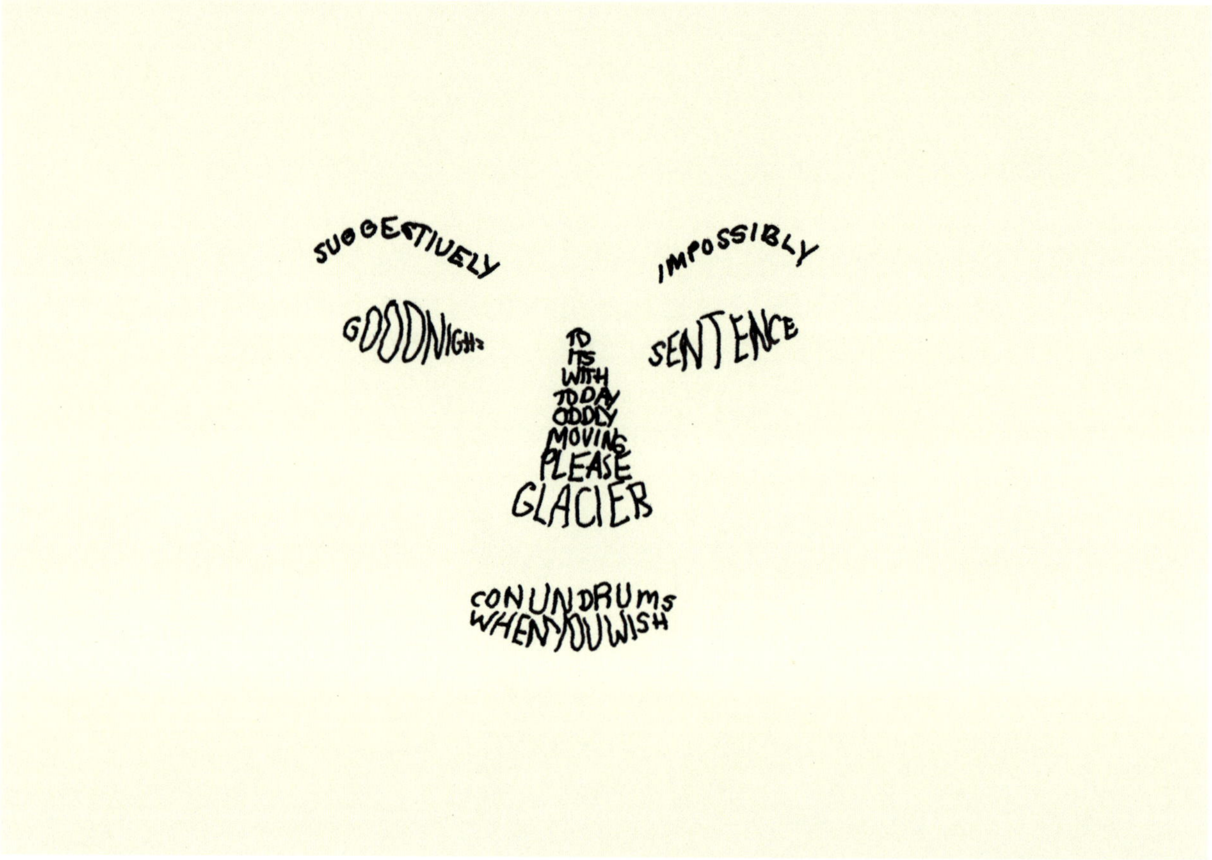

SUGGESTIVELY IMPOSSIBLY

GOODNIGHT SENTENCE

TO
ITS
WITH
TODAY
ODDLY
MOVING
PLEASE
GLACIER

CONUNDRUMS
WHEN YOU WISH

CONUNDRUMS WHEN YOU WISH

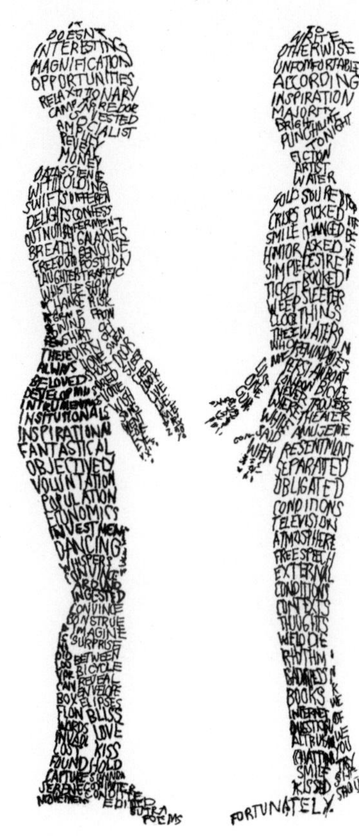

READING EACH OTHER

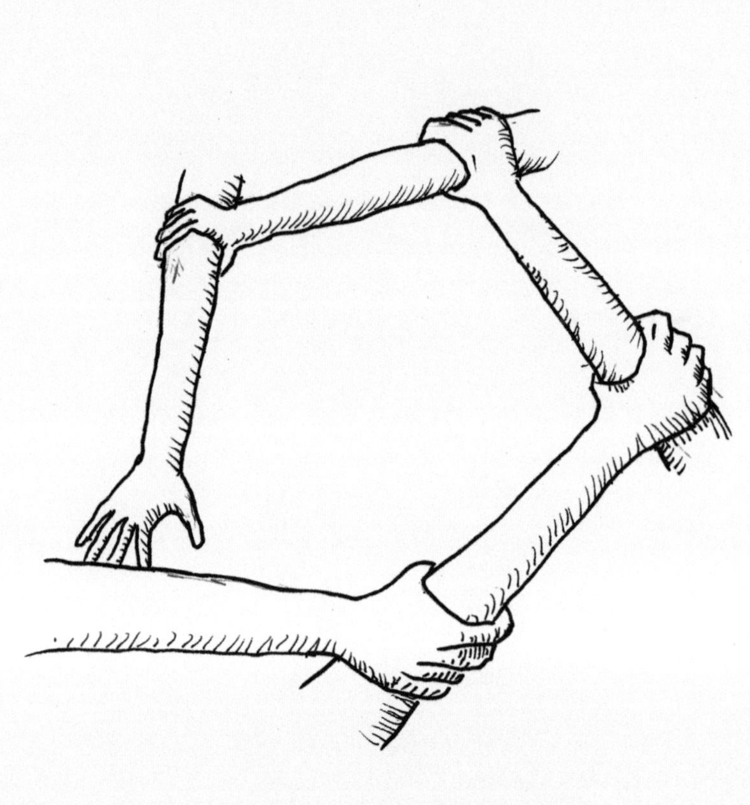

MUTUAL SUPPORT – MUTUAL RESTRAINT

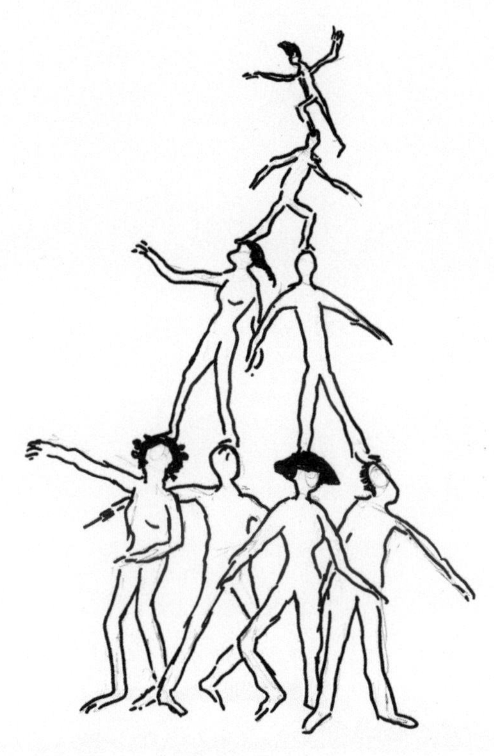

HIERARCHY

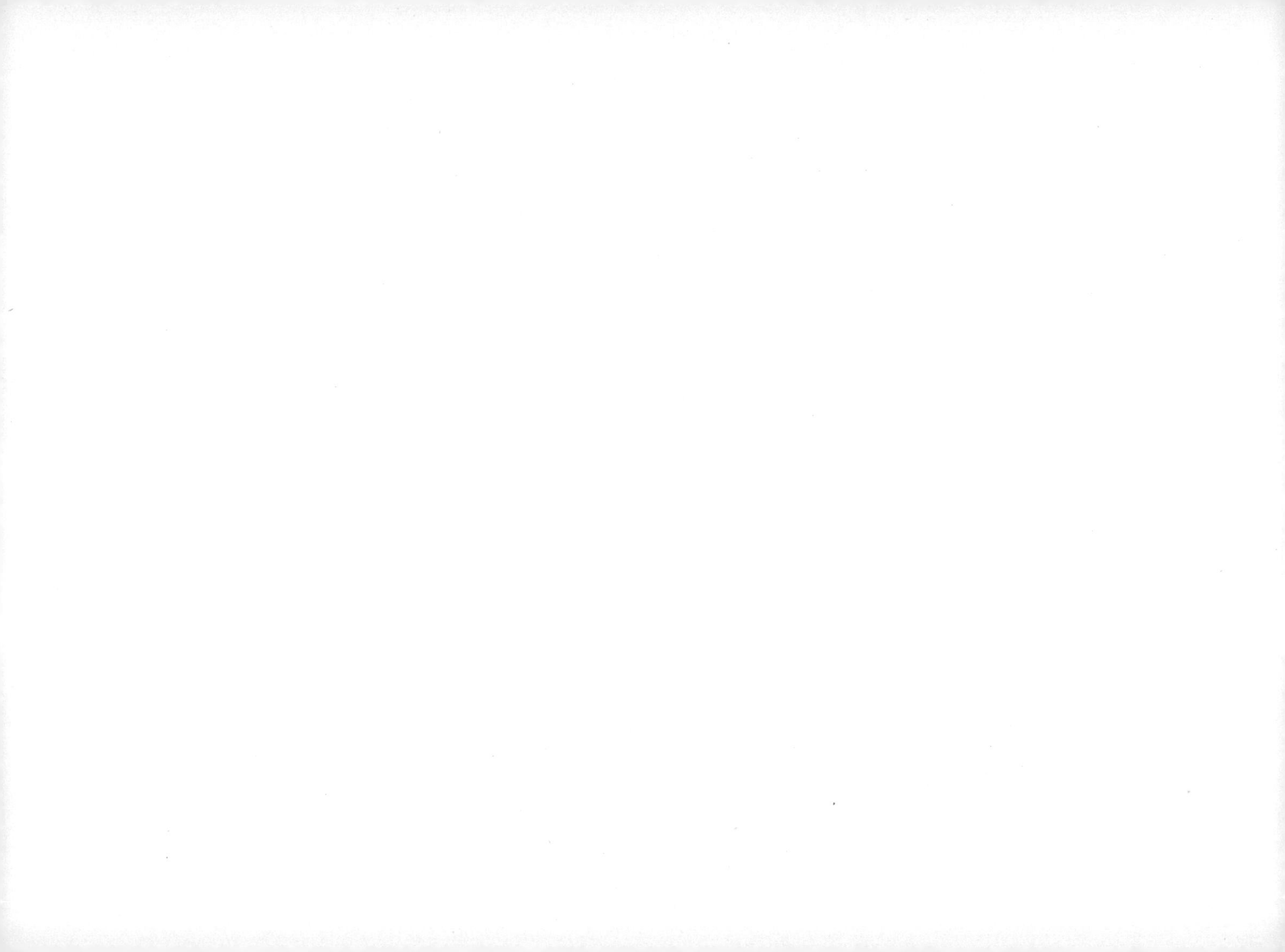

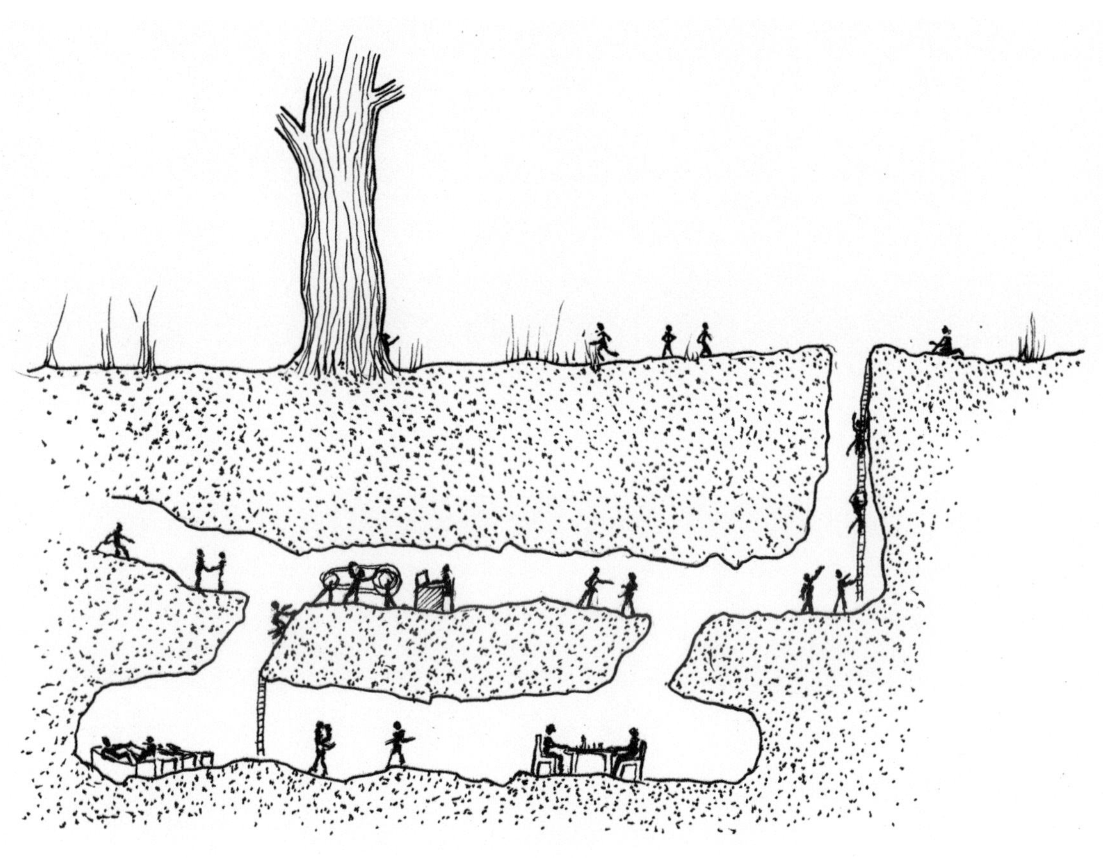

EUSOCIAL UTOPIA

PART FOUR

I CAN SEE BEYOND THE SWAMP!

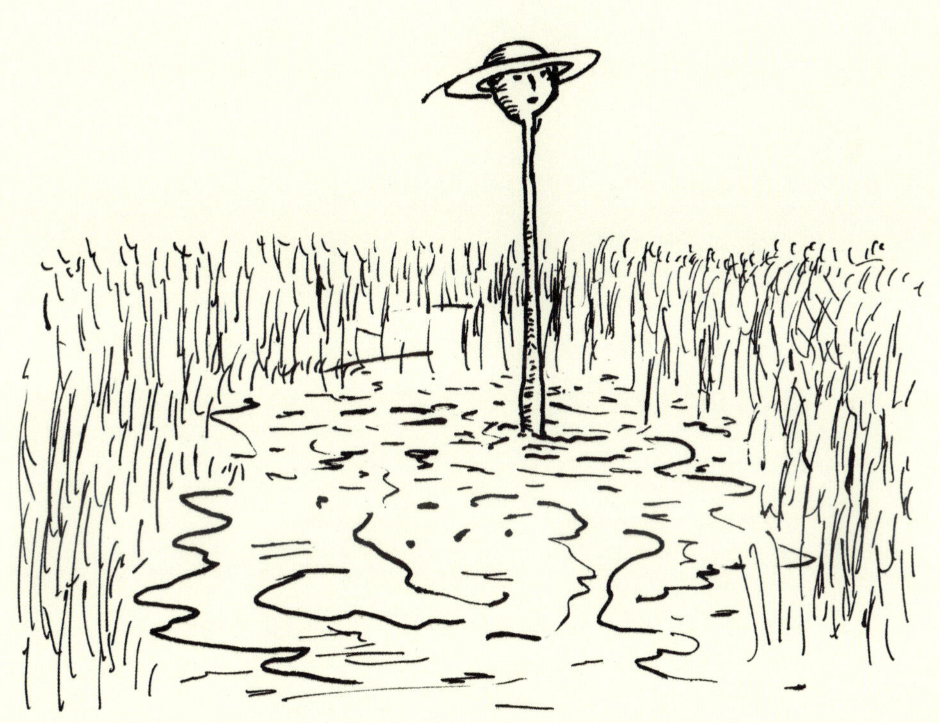

Here, from this slight rise,
I can see where the swamp ends.

The swamp is not the whole world!
Dare I go there?

We have the possibility of movement
and we are in the process, transported.

What might happen?
What lies beyond?
Beyond our village,
beyond our network.
Can we go there?
Beyond our selves?

I can see it!
It is better than what is here.
I need a way to get there.
To move who I thought I was.

Can I bring my friends with me?
Is it expensive?
Will I know how to be there?
Can I fit in?
Will they like me there?

There's no going back, eh?

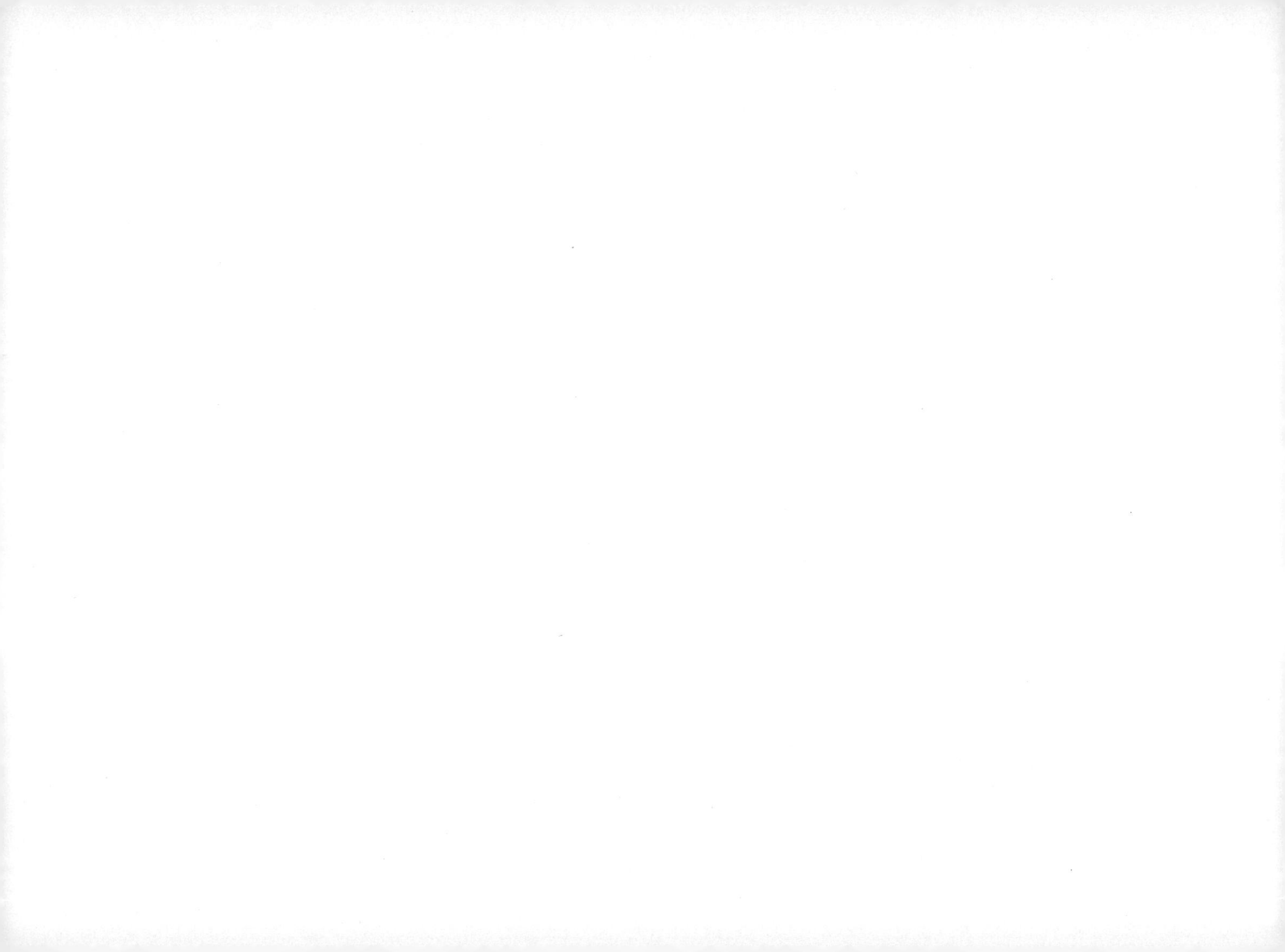

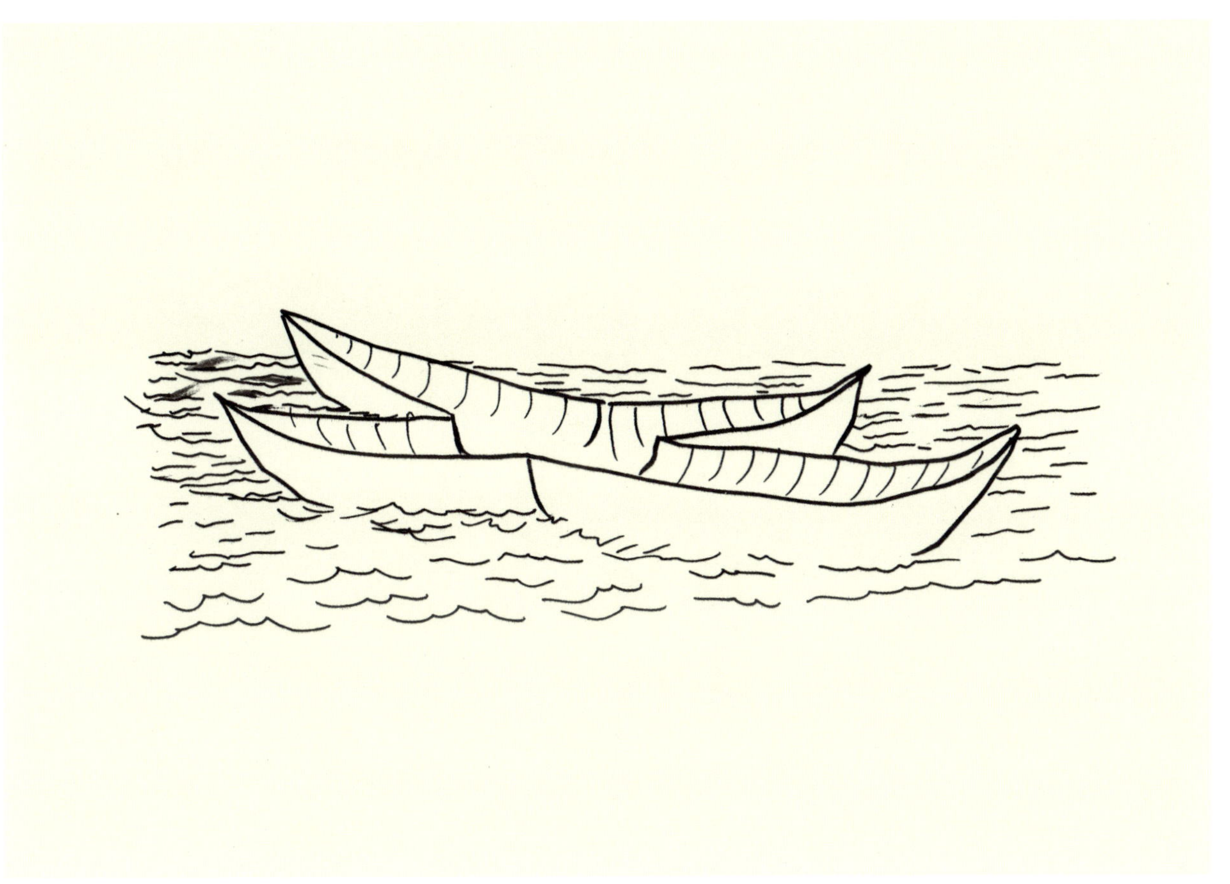

FOUR-WAY BOAT

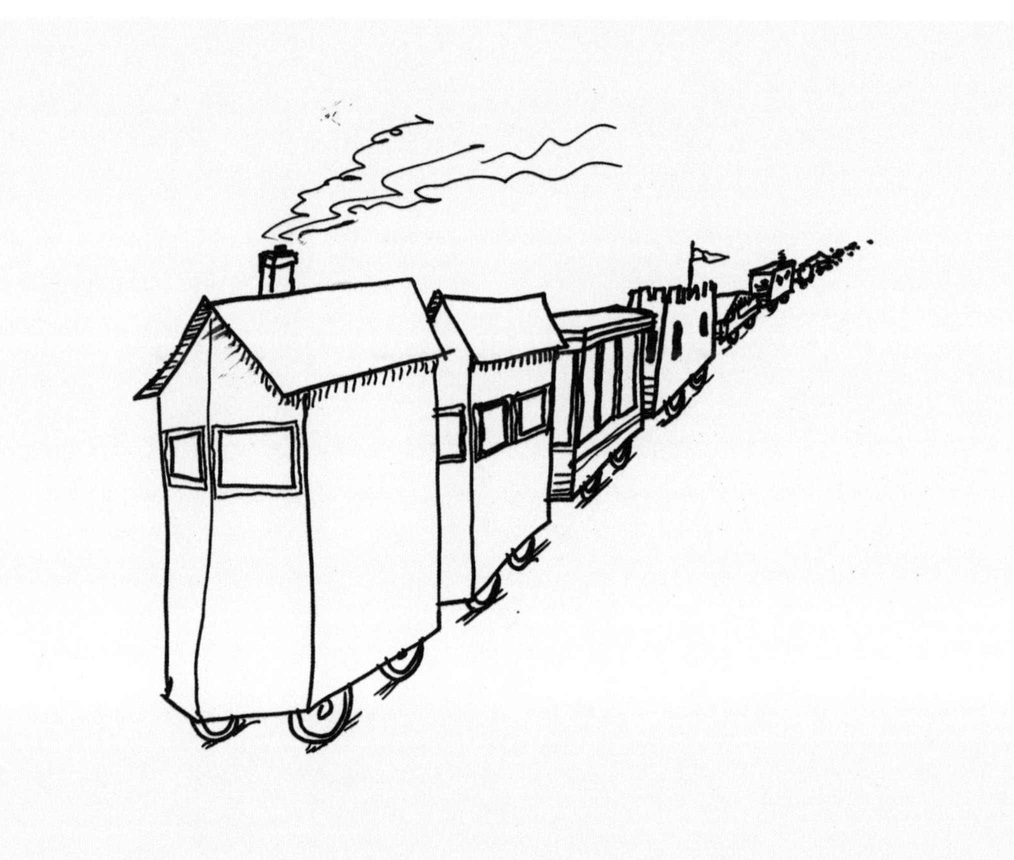

MOVING DAY!

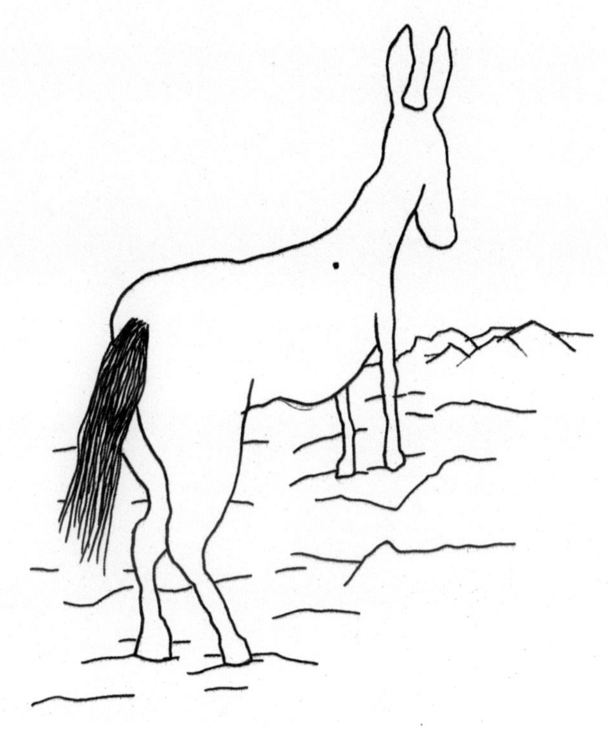

A PIMPLE ON MY ASS

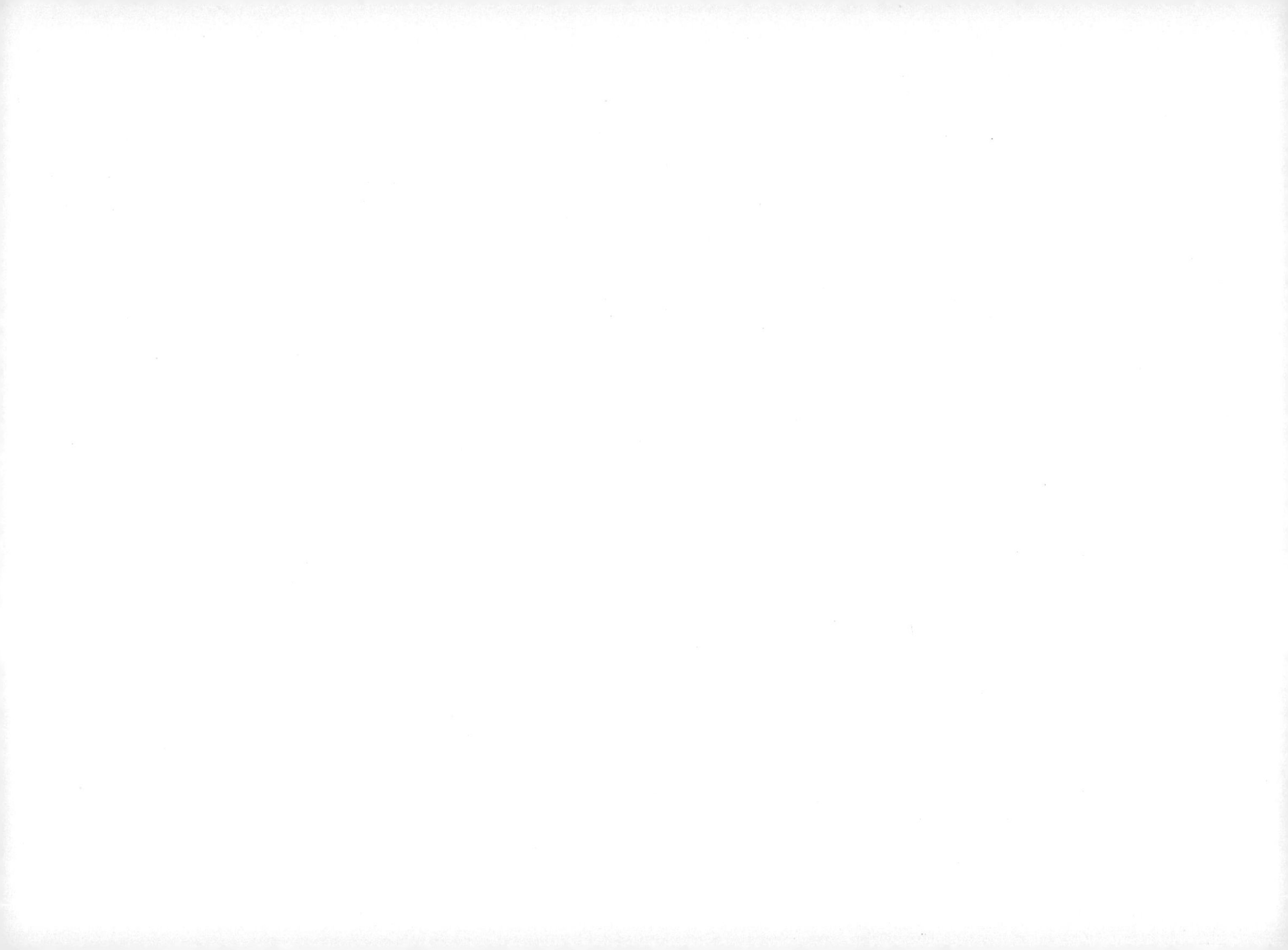

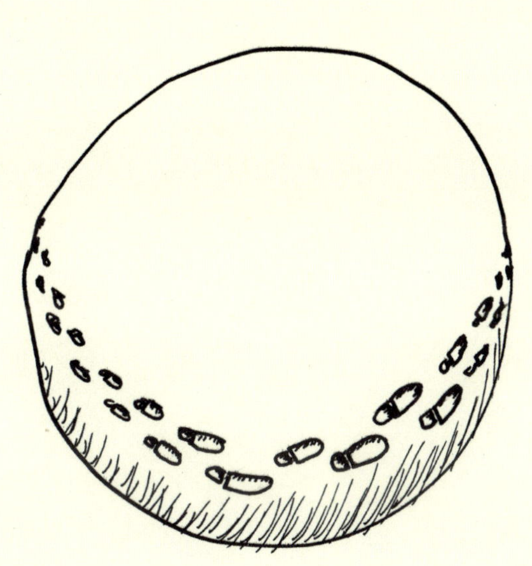

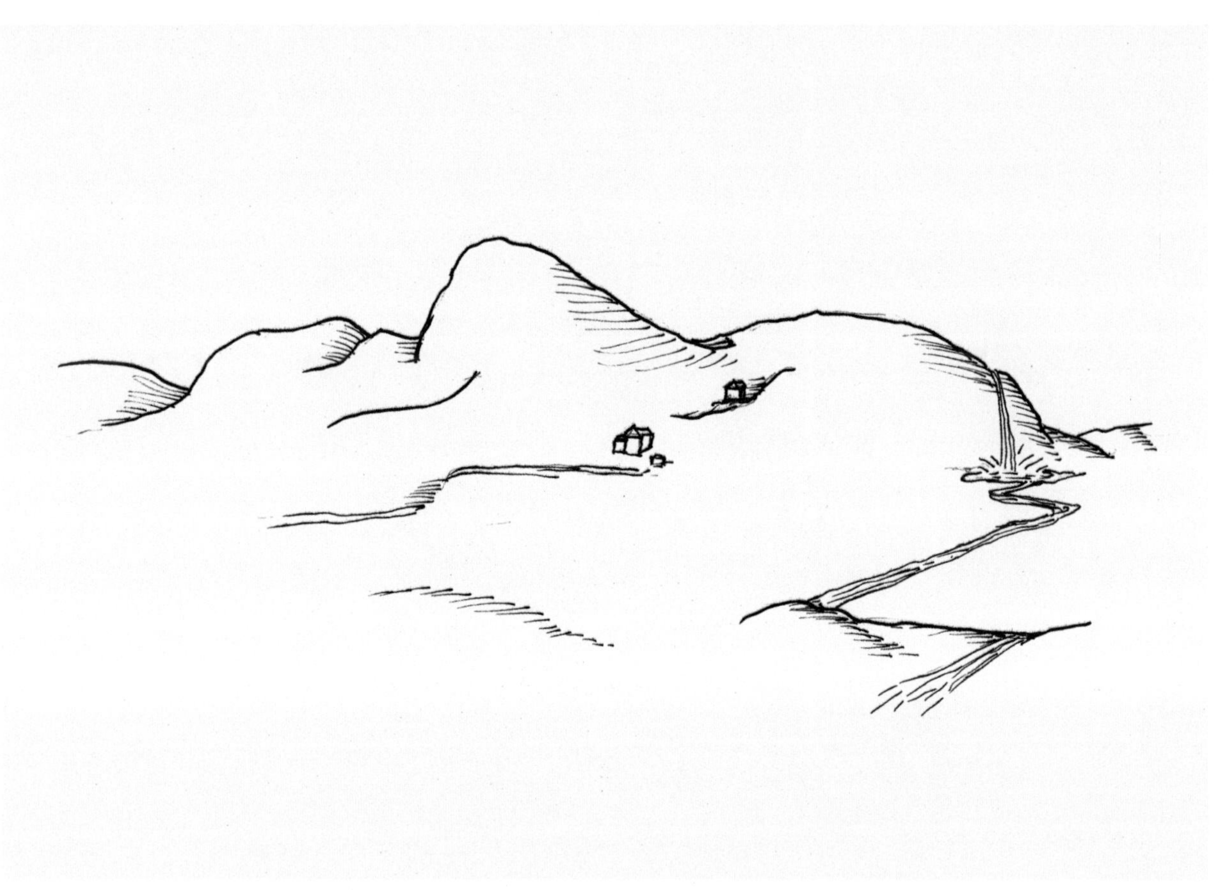

NATURE MAN

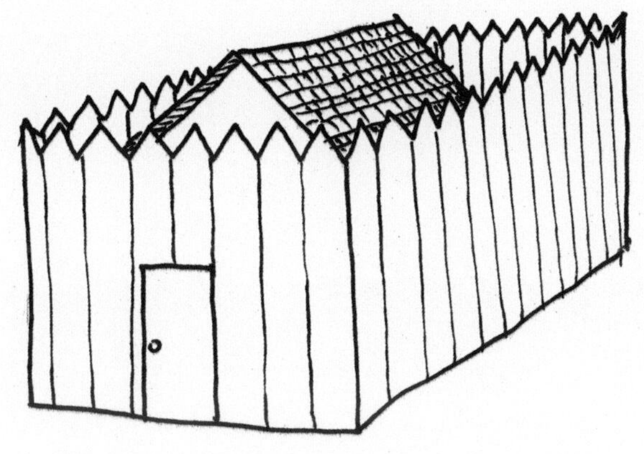

SAFE AS HOUSES

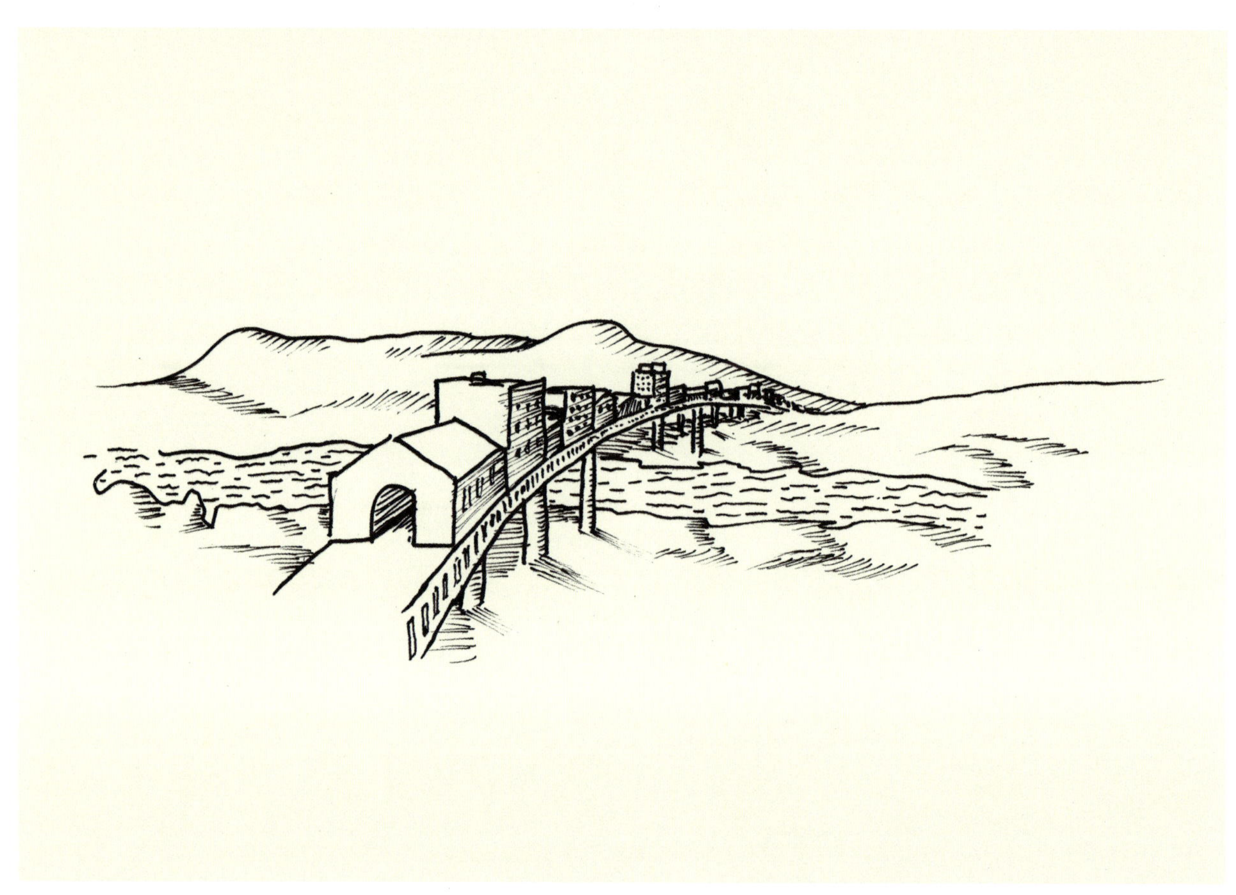

NEITHER HERE NOR THERE

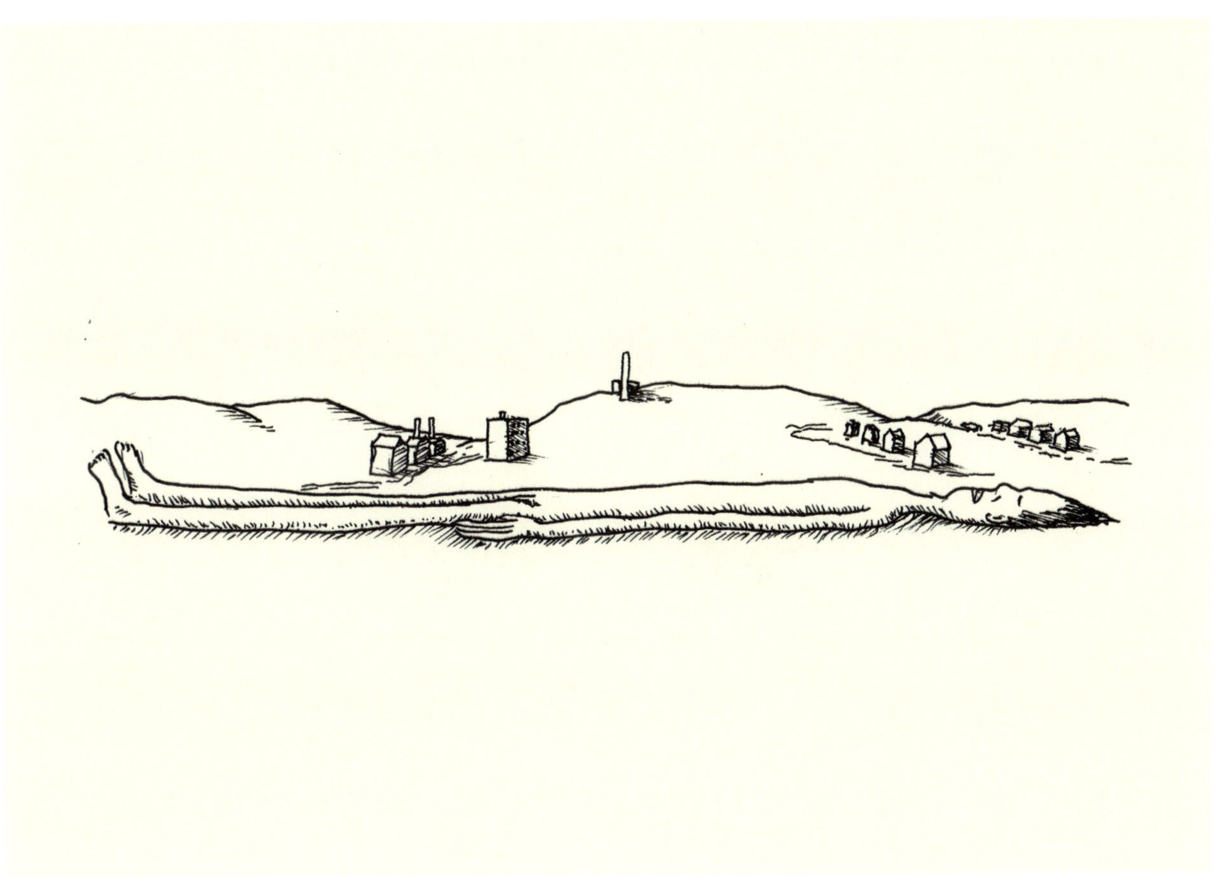

THE LONG BODY

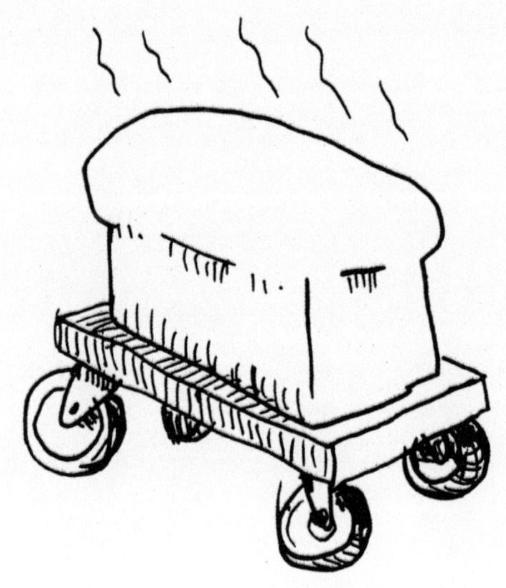

HOT BREAD DELIVERY

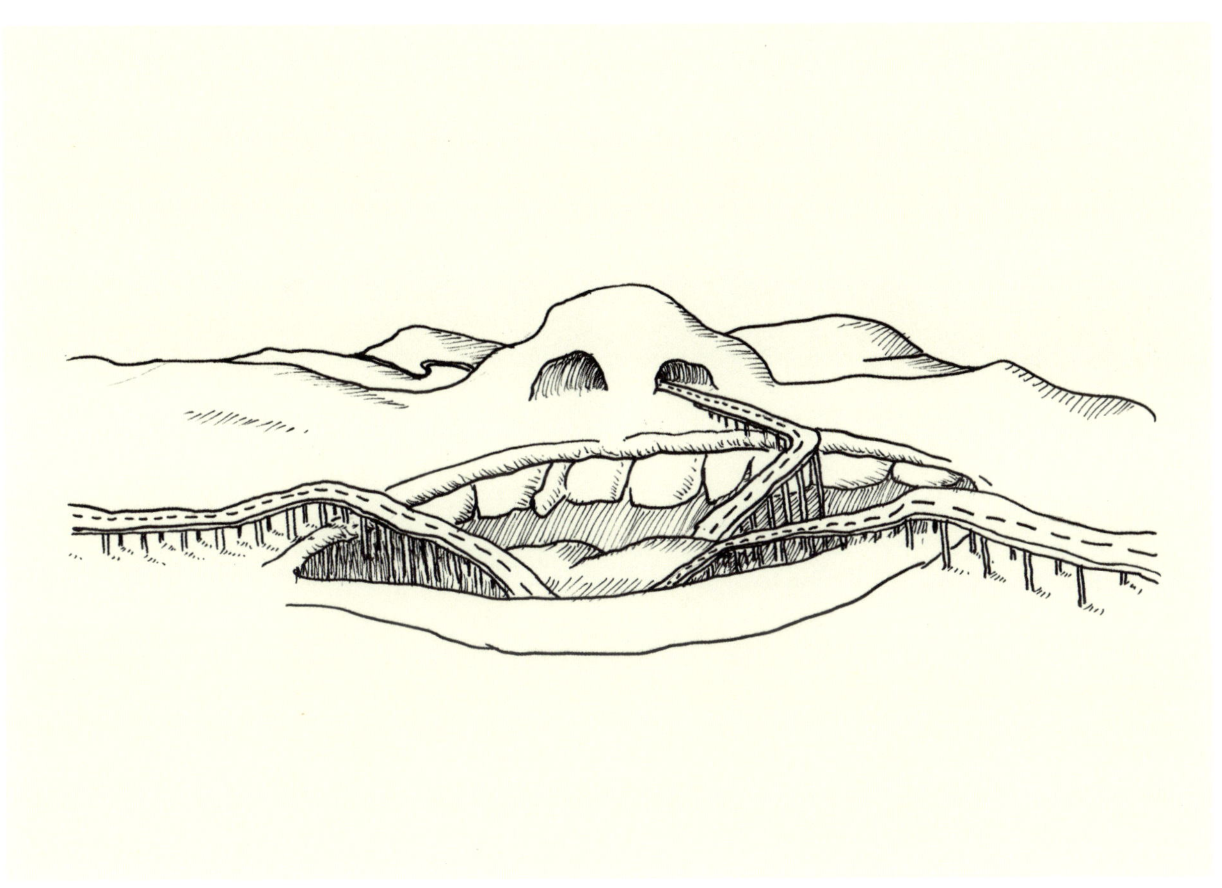

DRIVE IN

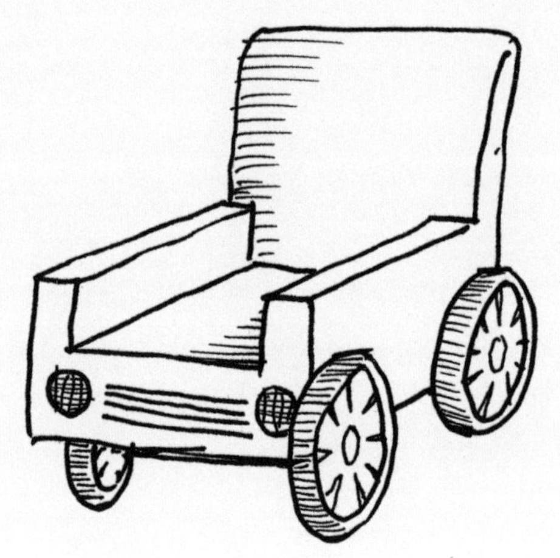

PERSONAL LUXURY TRANSPORT

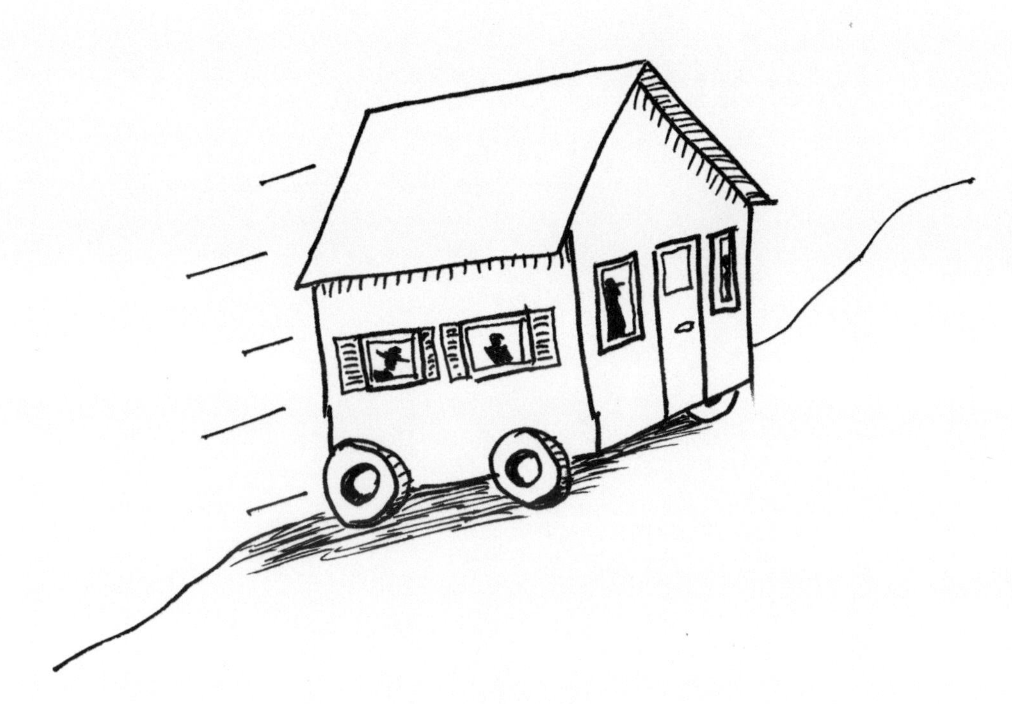

MOVIN' ON UP

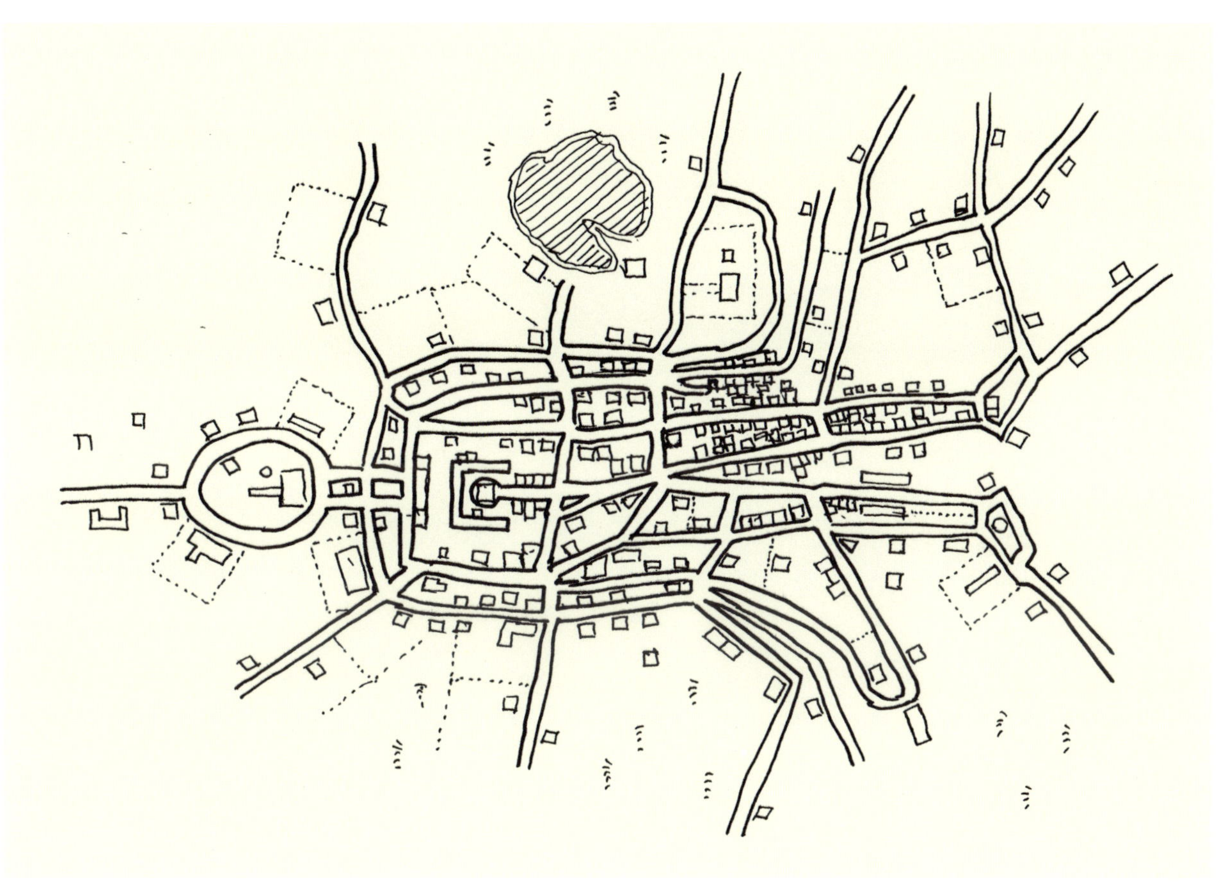

THE VILLAGE BODY

PART FIVE

CITYHEAD

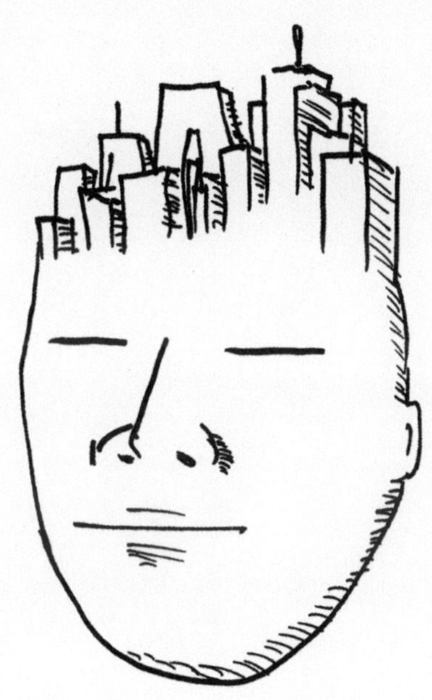

We live in a city in our heads.
The buildings that surround us,
along with our clothes and our hairstyles,
we invented these things.

Like termite mounds, they mirror, reflect, and amplify our assumptions and thoughts and our unacknowledged social structures.
As inside, so outside.

The cities are fantastic and beautiful. A world of places, people, and things, moments real and imagined, all jostle for space in there.

People with prodigious memories decorate memory palaces and file their moments along streets and boulevards. These markers are invisible to others but as real as anything else to the inhabitants. A literal stroll down memory lane.

Everything in its right place,
labeled and grouped
according to elaborate and ever-changing criteria.

Only you can find the way—in the city in your head.

We replicate and impose these ways of categorizing and naming things on the outside world. Our template is our guard against chaos and an ever-changing filter.

The categories offer us both liberation and confinement.
Geometries of freedom and hierarchies of restriction.
Chaotic and organized,
passionate and dissolute.

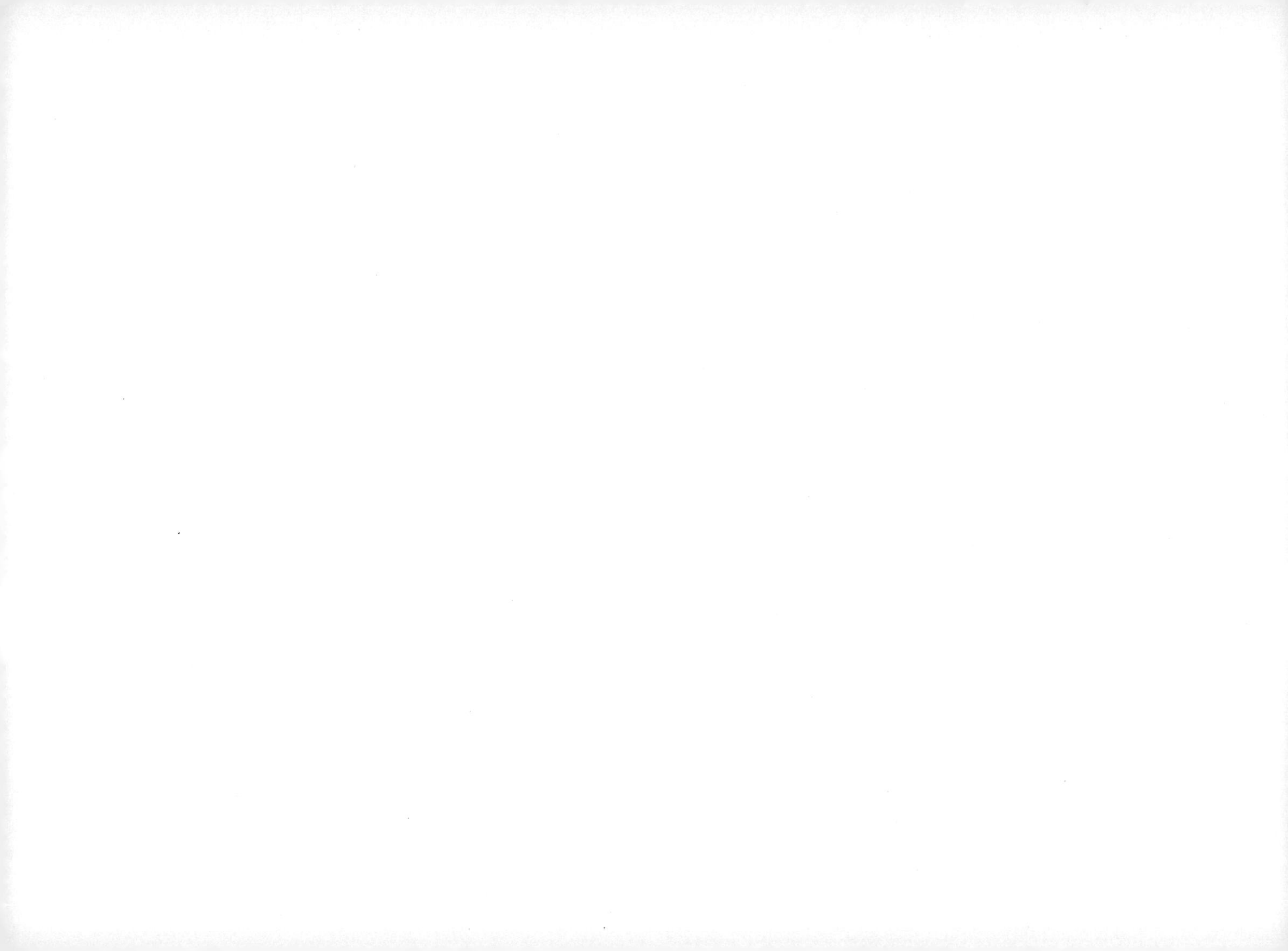

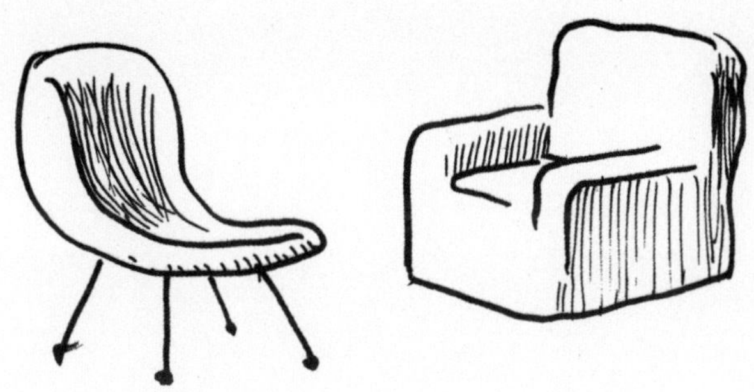

FRIENDS

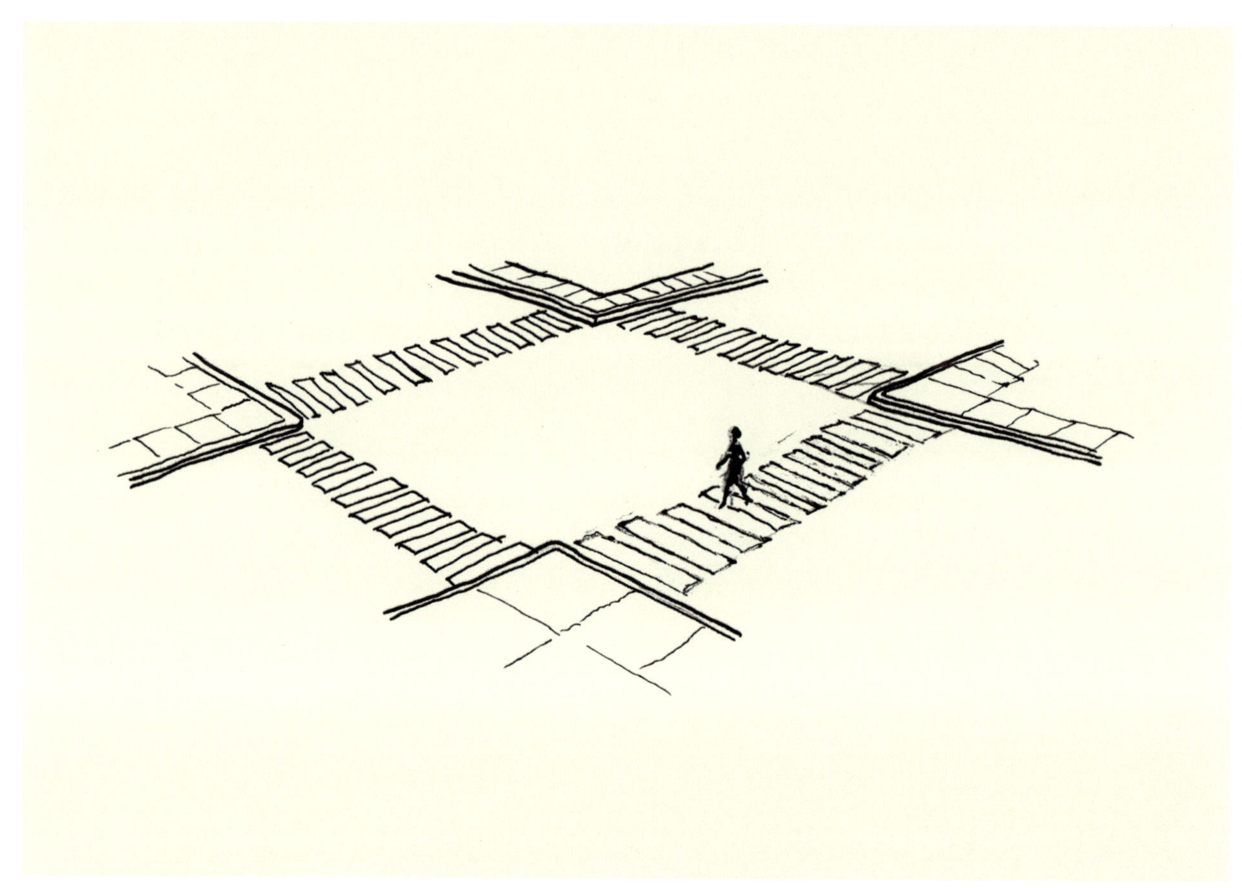

TO GET TO THE OTHER SIDE

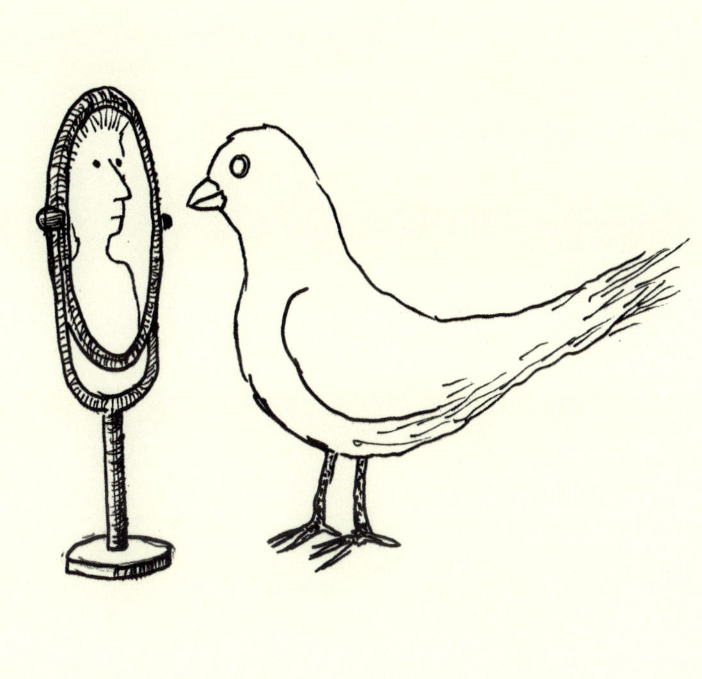

WHO'S A PRETTY BOY THEN ?

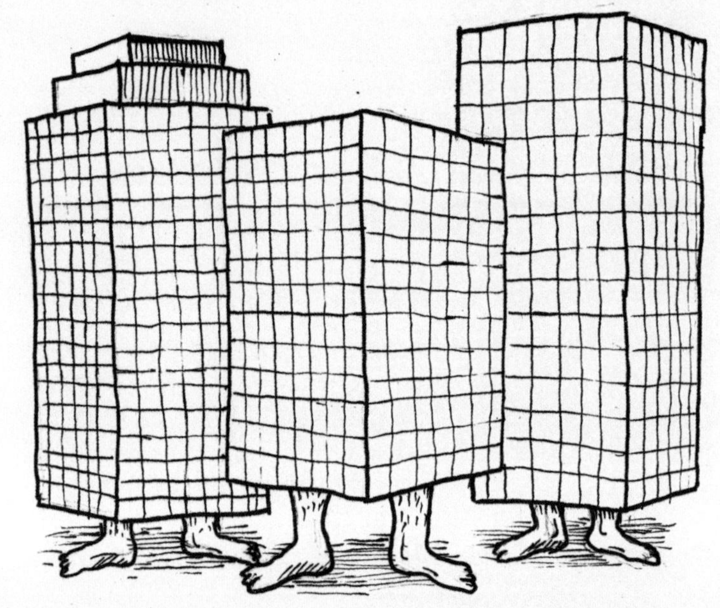

DEVELOPMENT

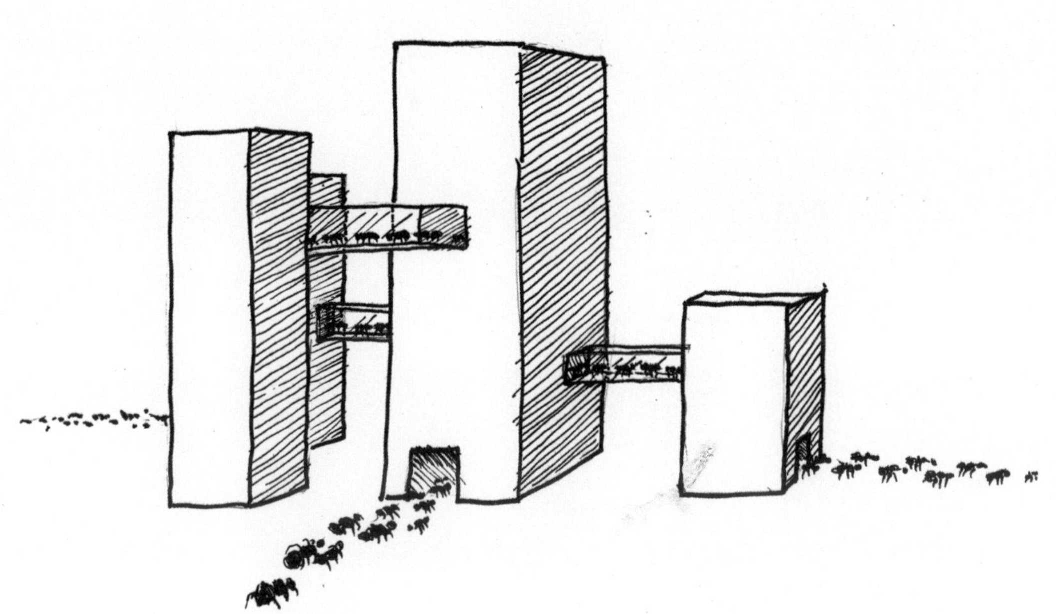

LIFE IS GOOD

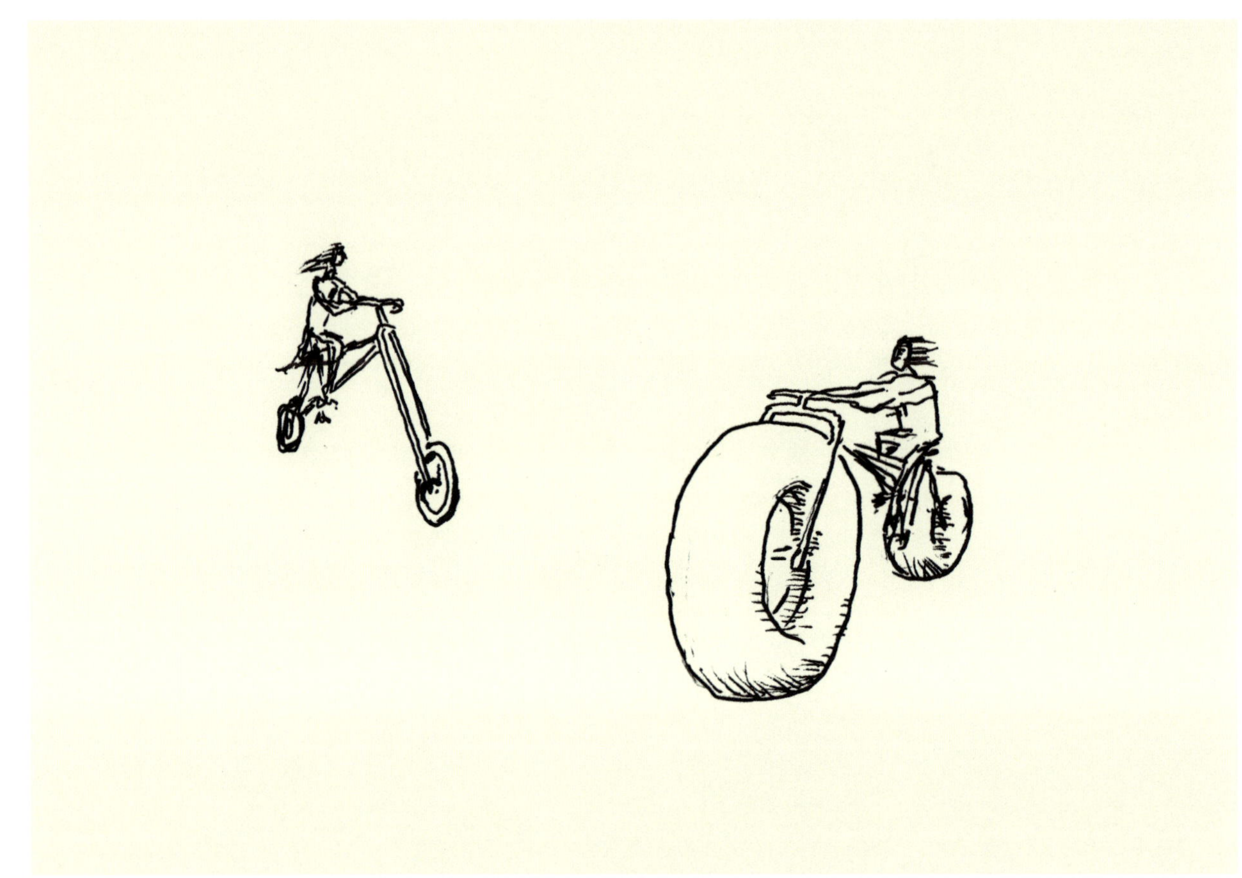

VELO OPTIONS

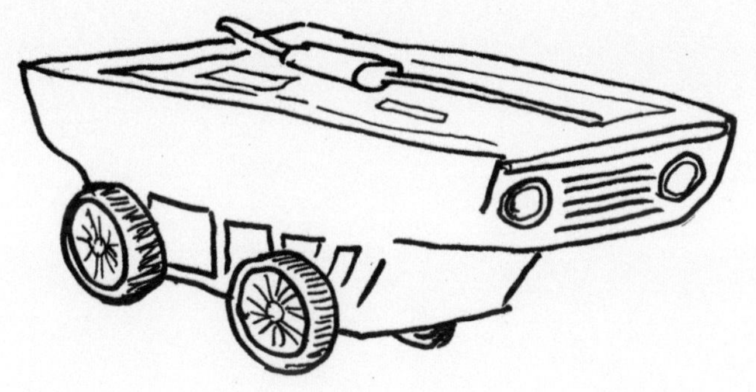

ANTIPODES CAR

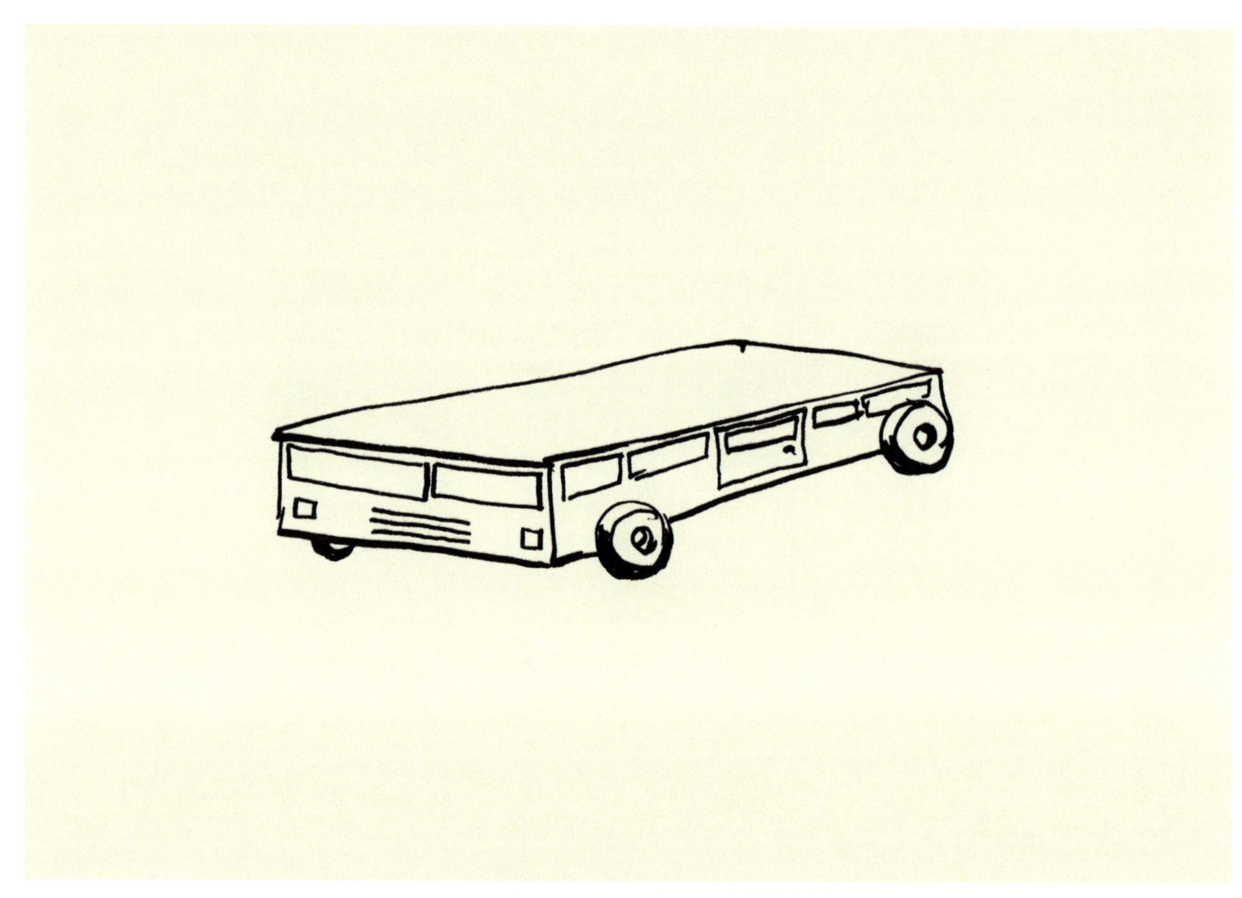

CAR PLATFORM

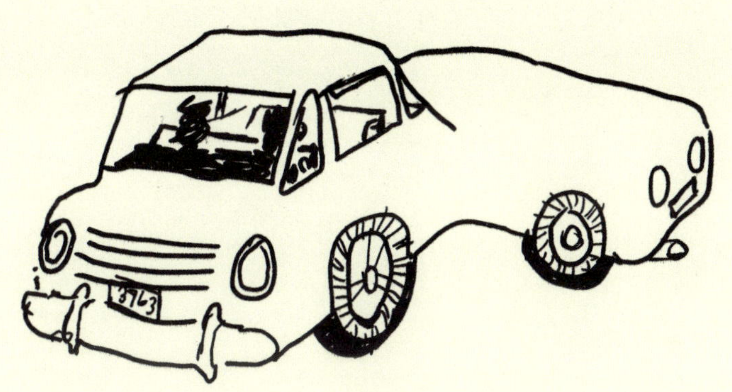
3763

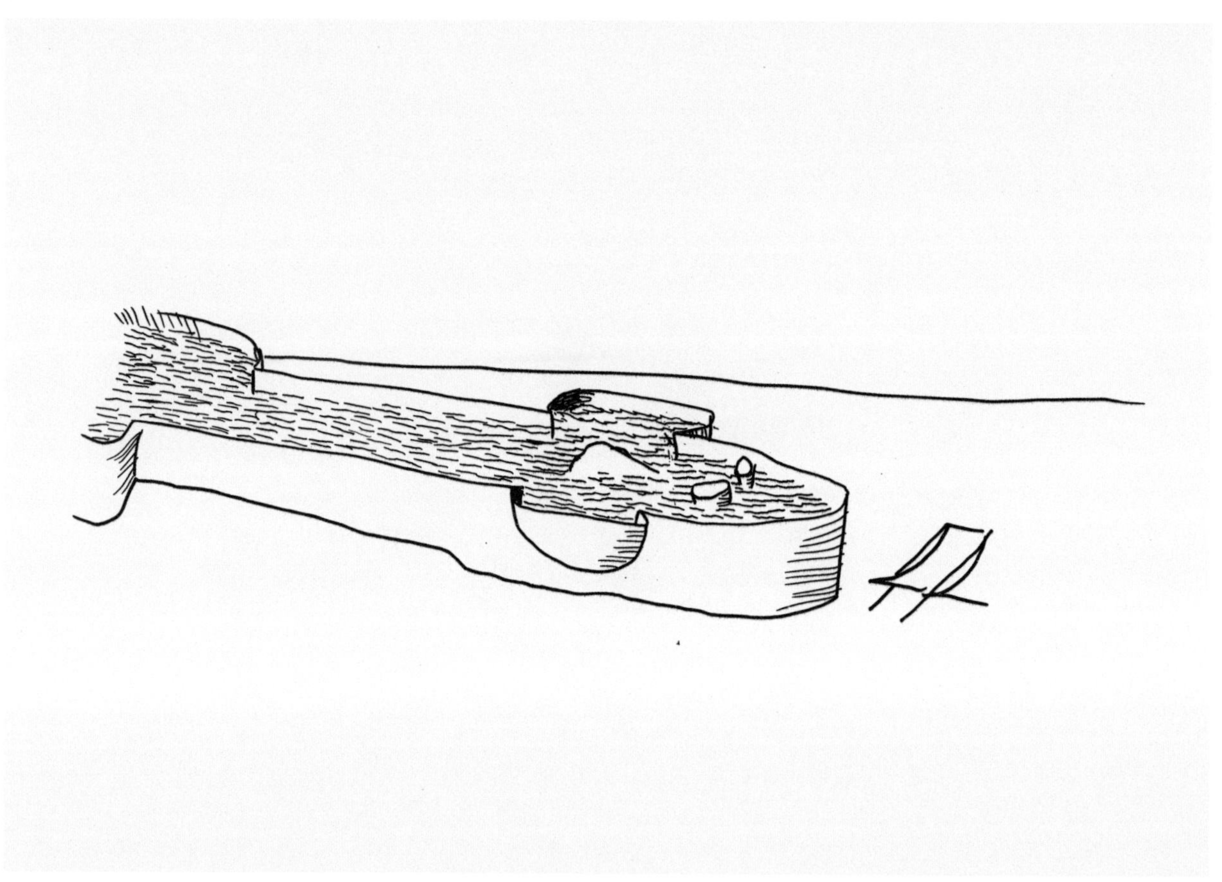

SWIM INSIDE MY HEAD

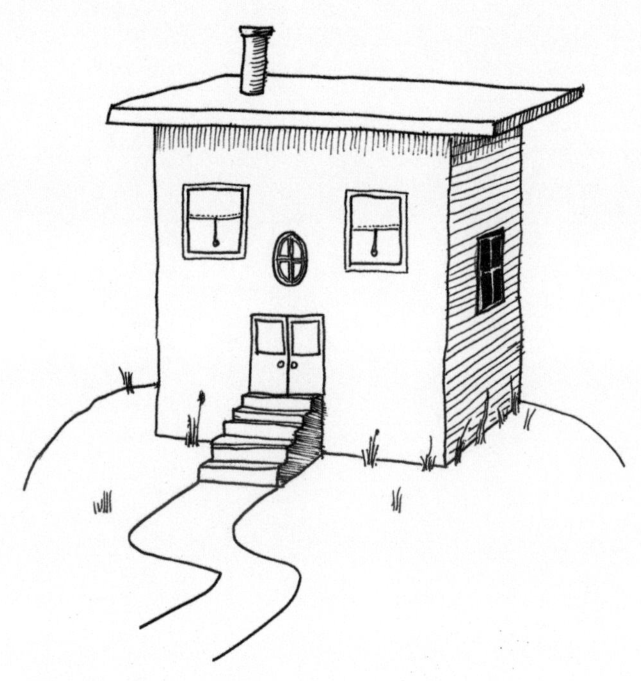

LIVIN' IN MY HEAD

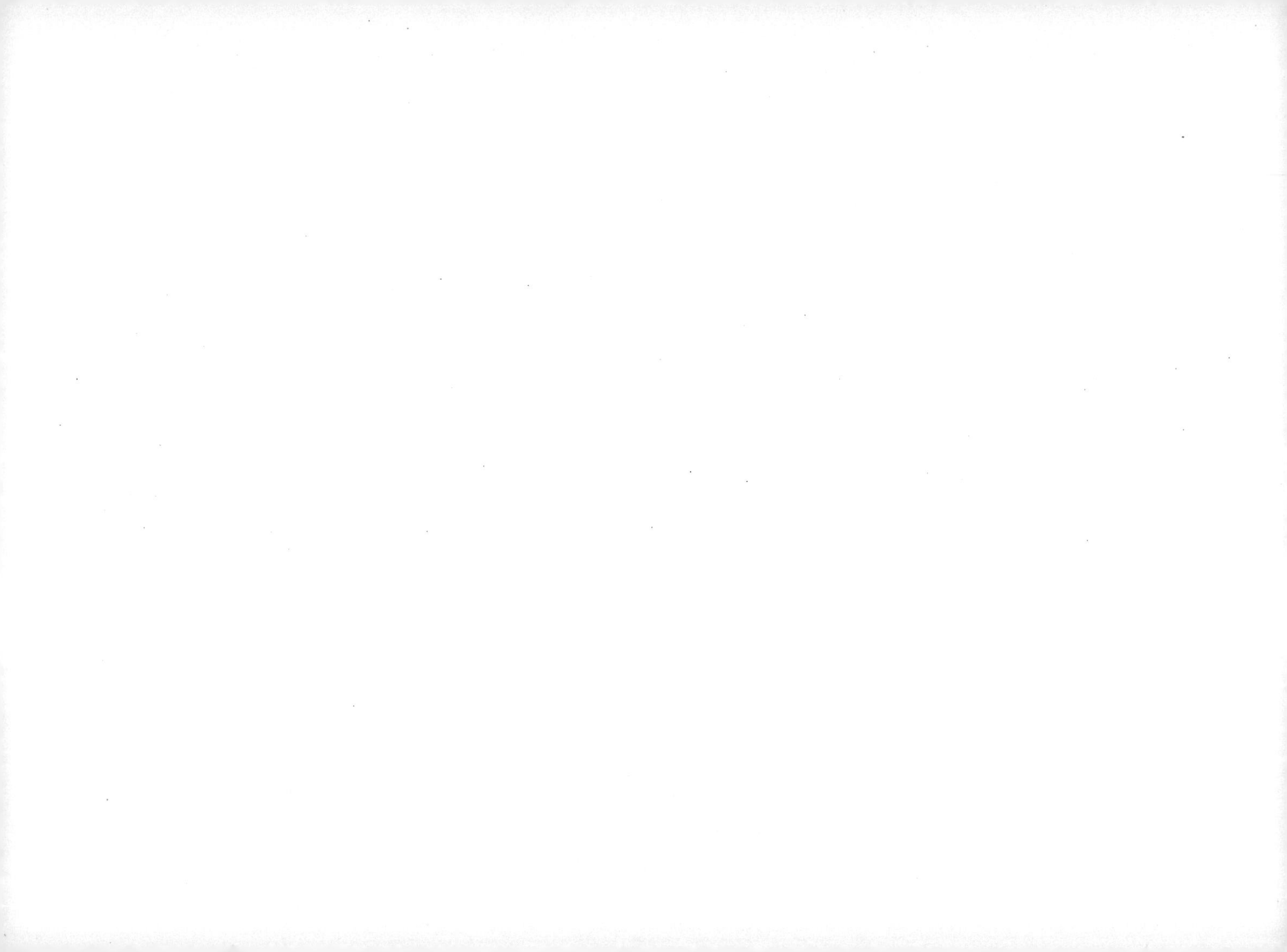

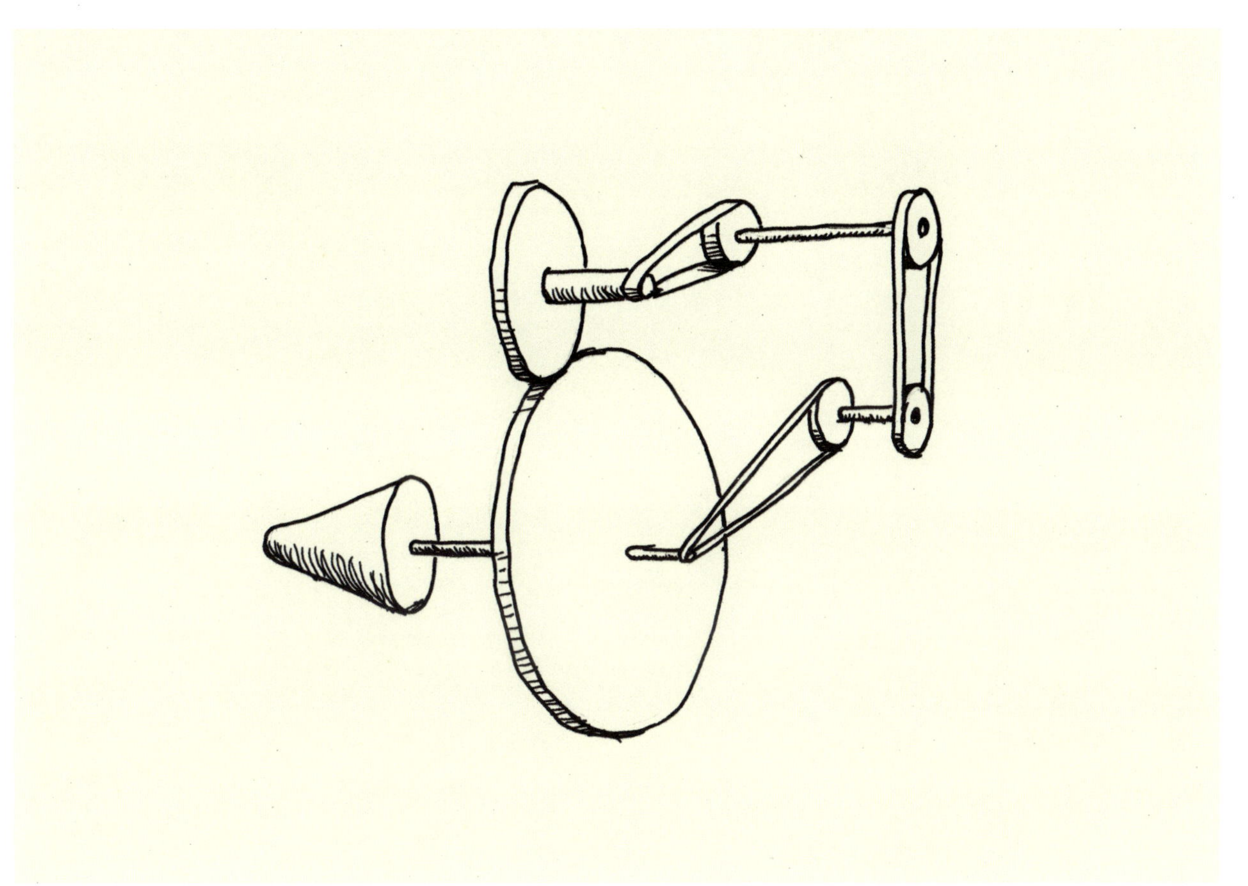

WHEEL OF FORTUNE

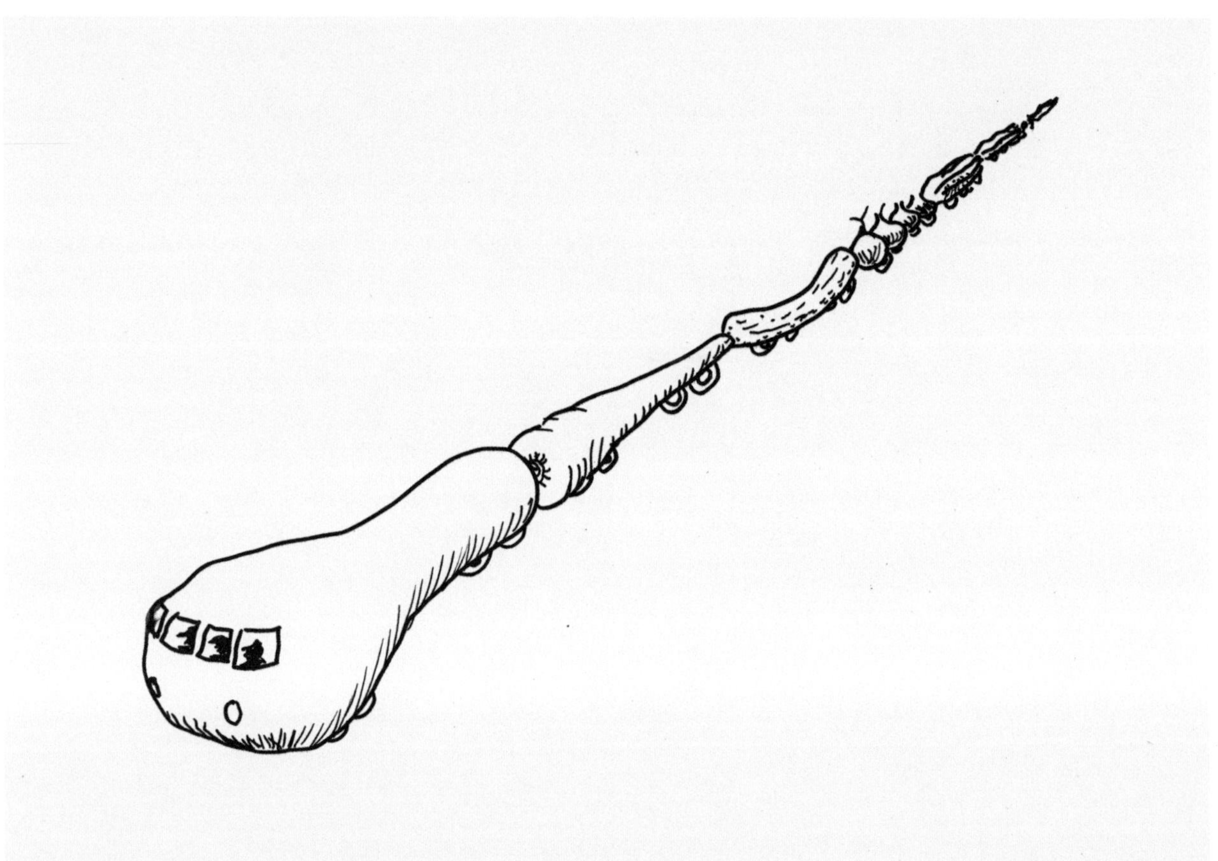

SUPPLY CHAIN

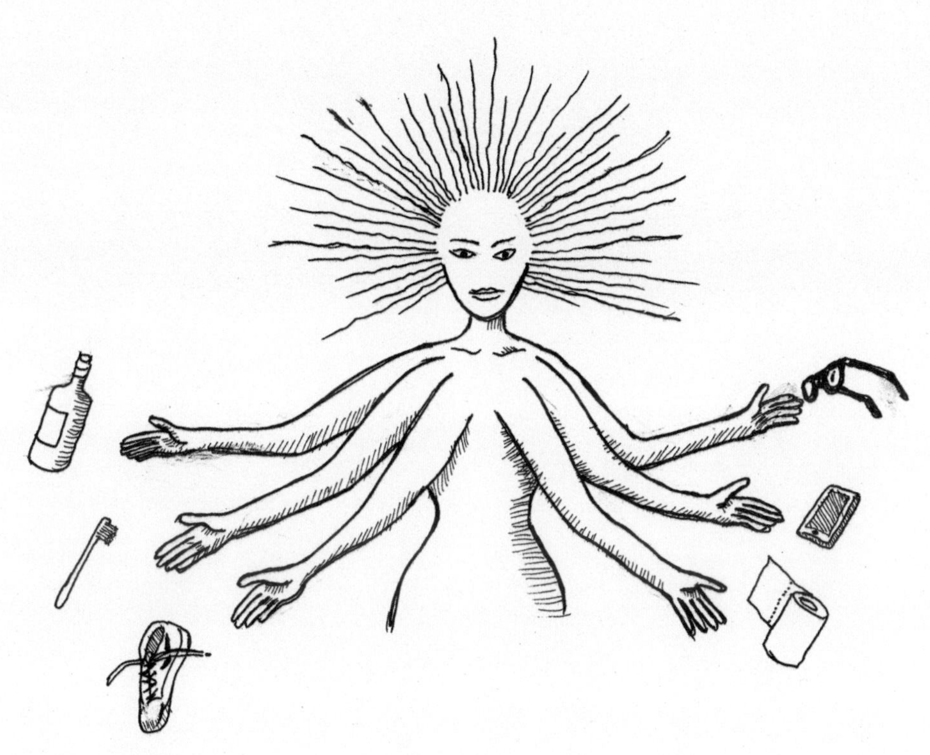

BESTOWER OF GIFTS

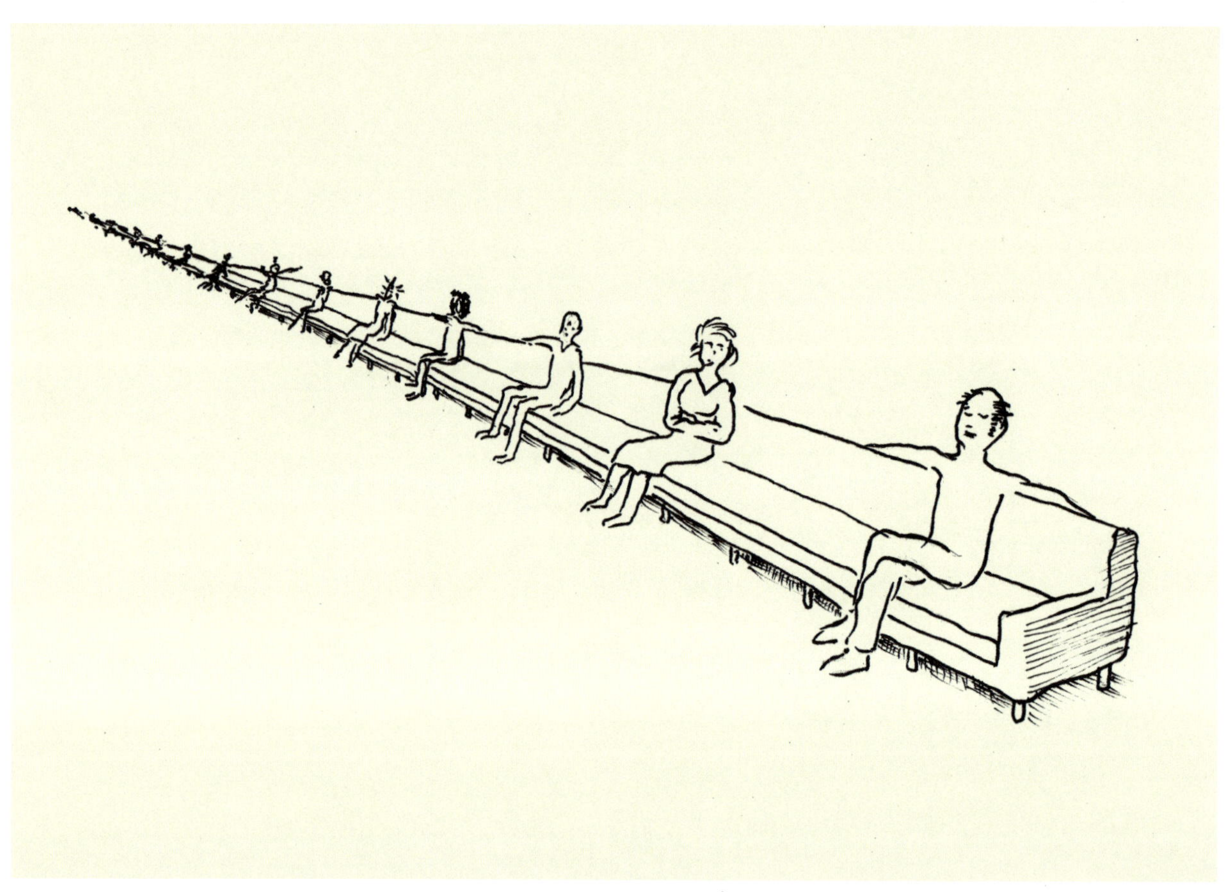

INFINITE SOFA

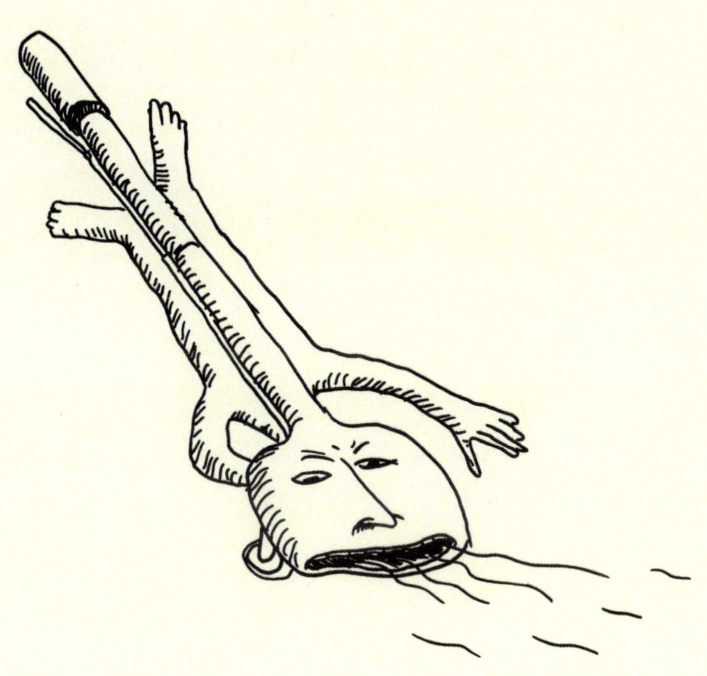

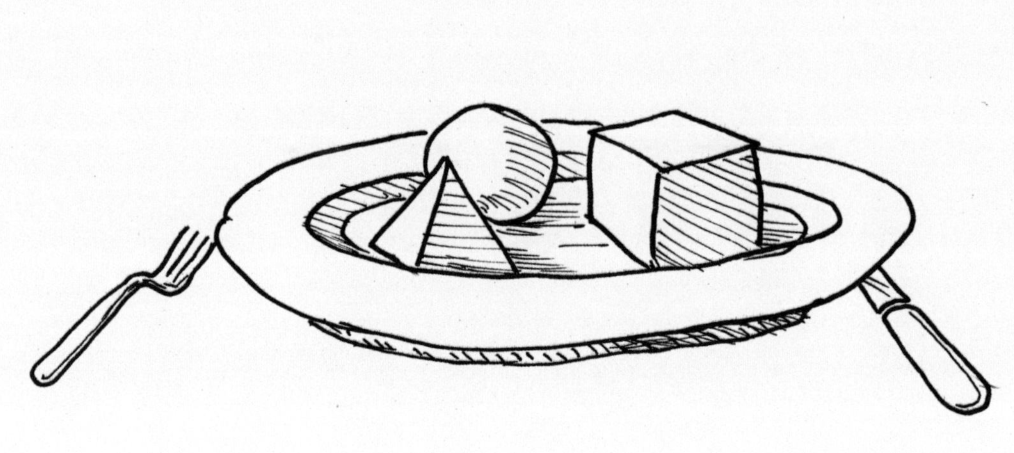

THE 3 FOOD GROUPS

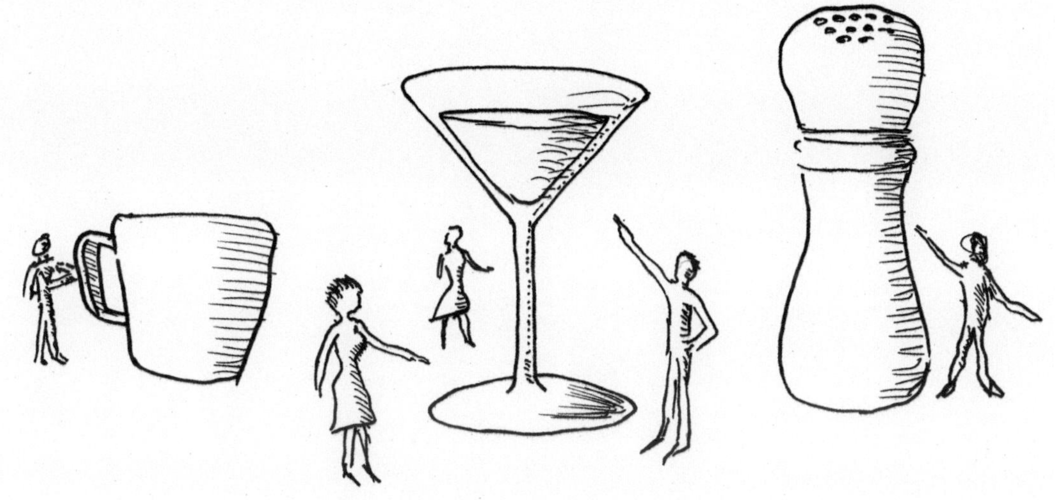

TABLETOP ADVENTURES

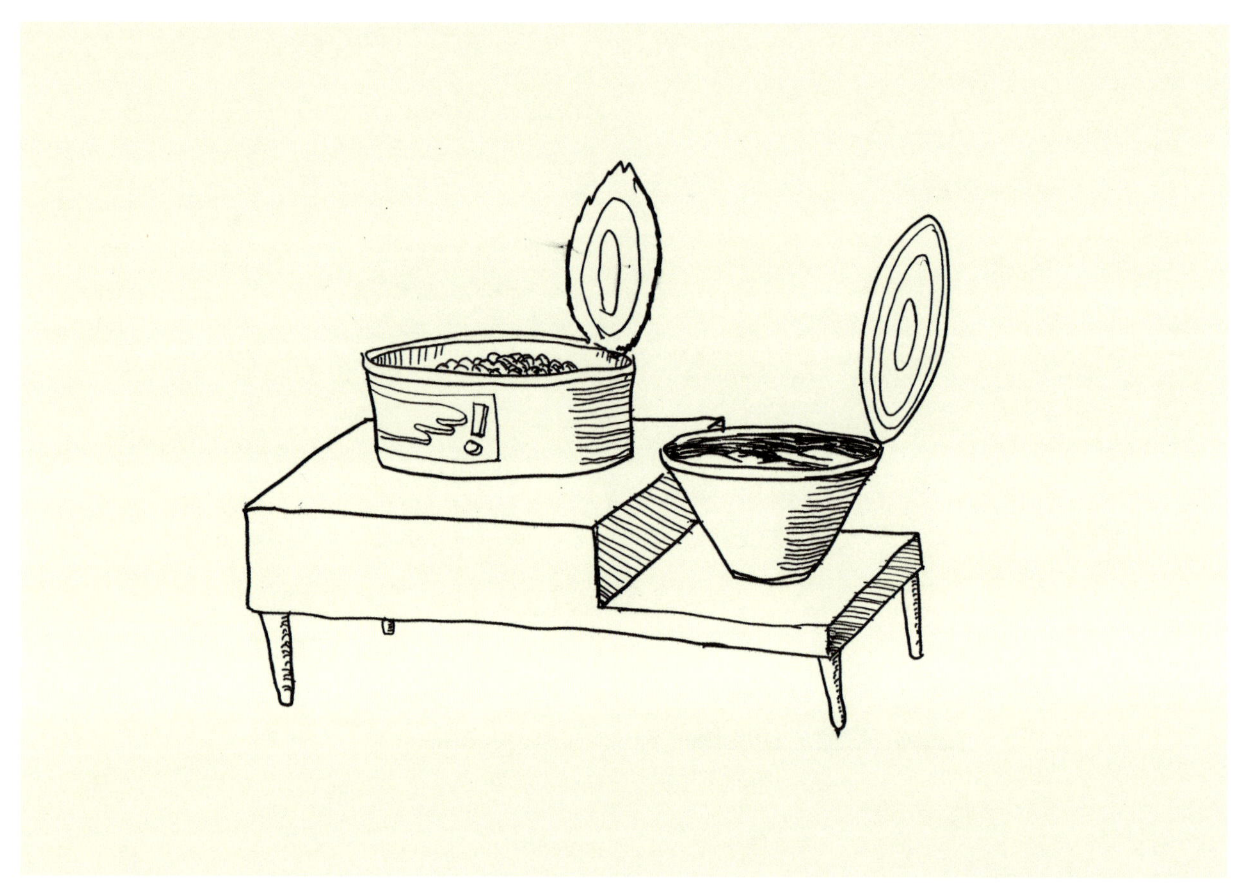

THE WINNERS!

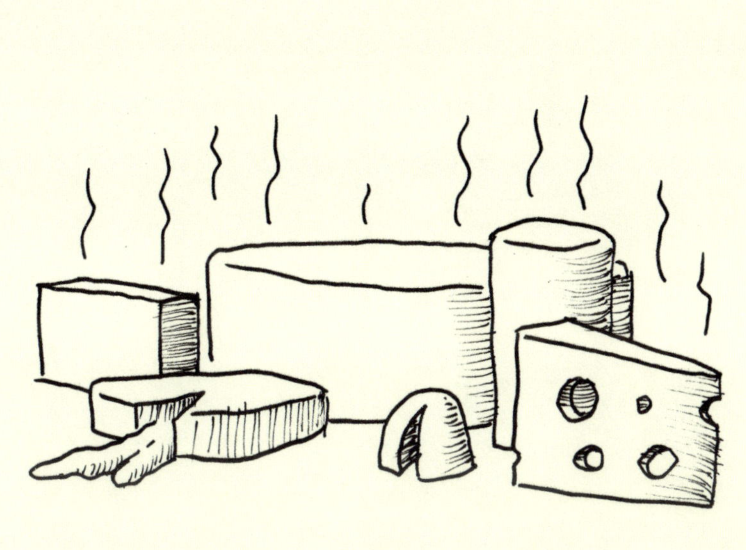

THE CHEESE STANDS ALONE

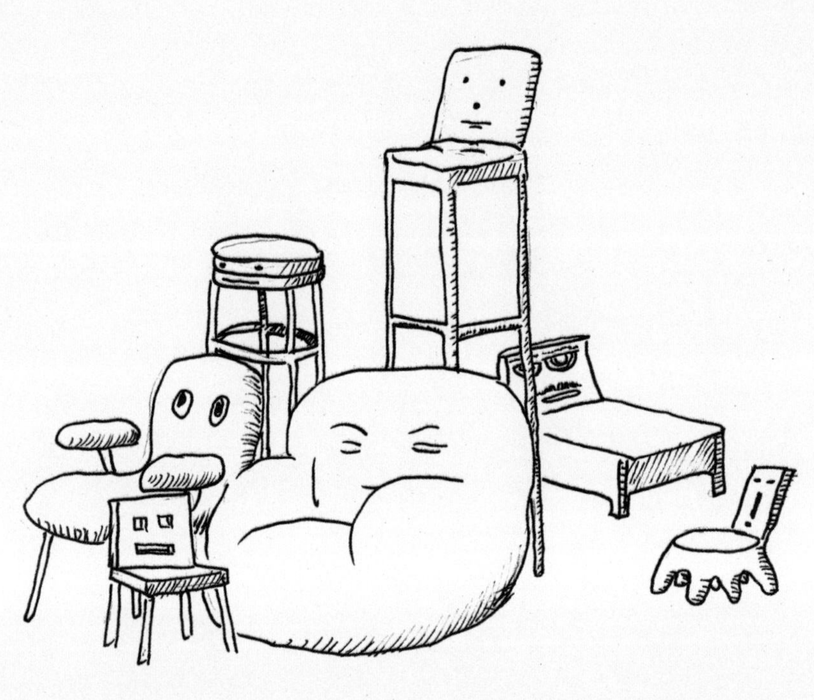

FAMILY PORTRAIT

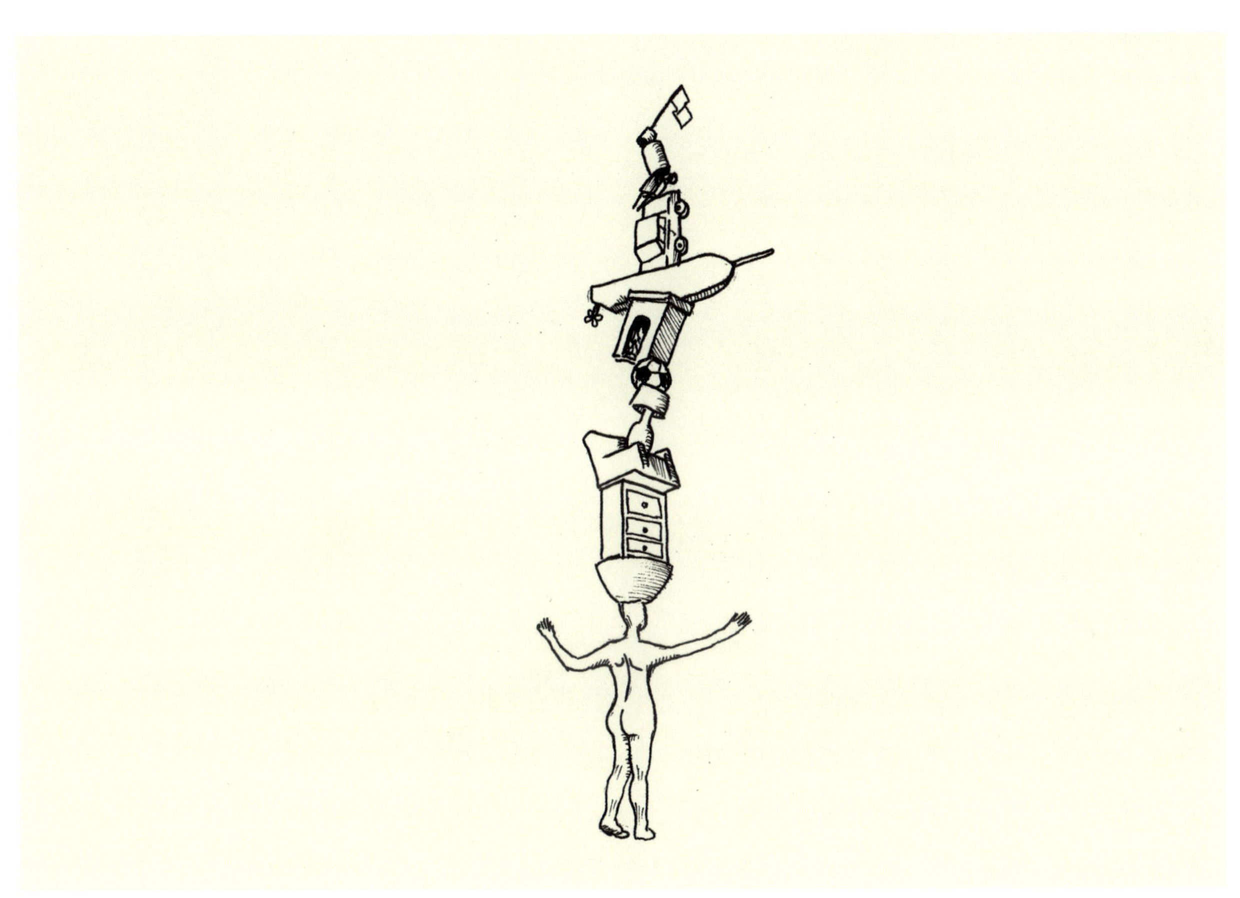

A BALANCED LIFE

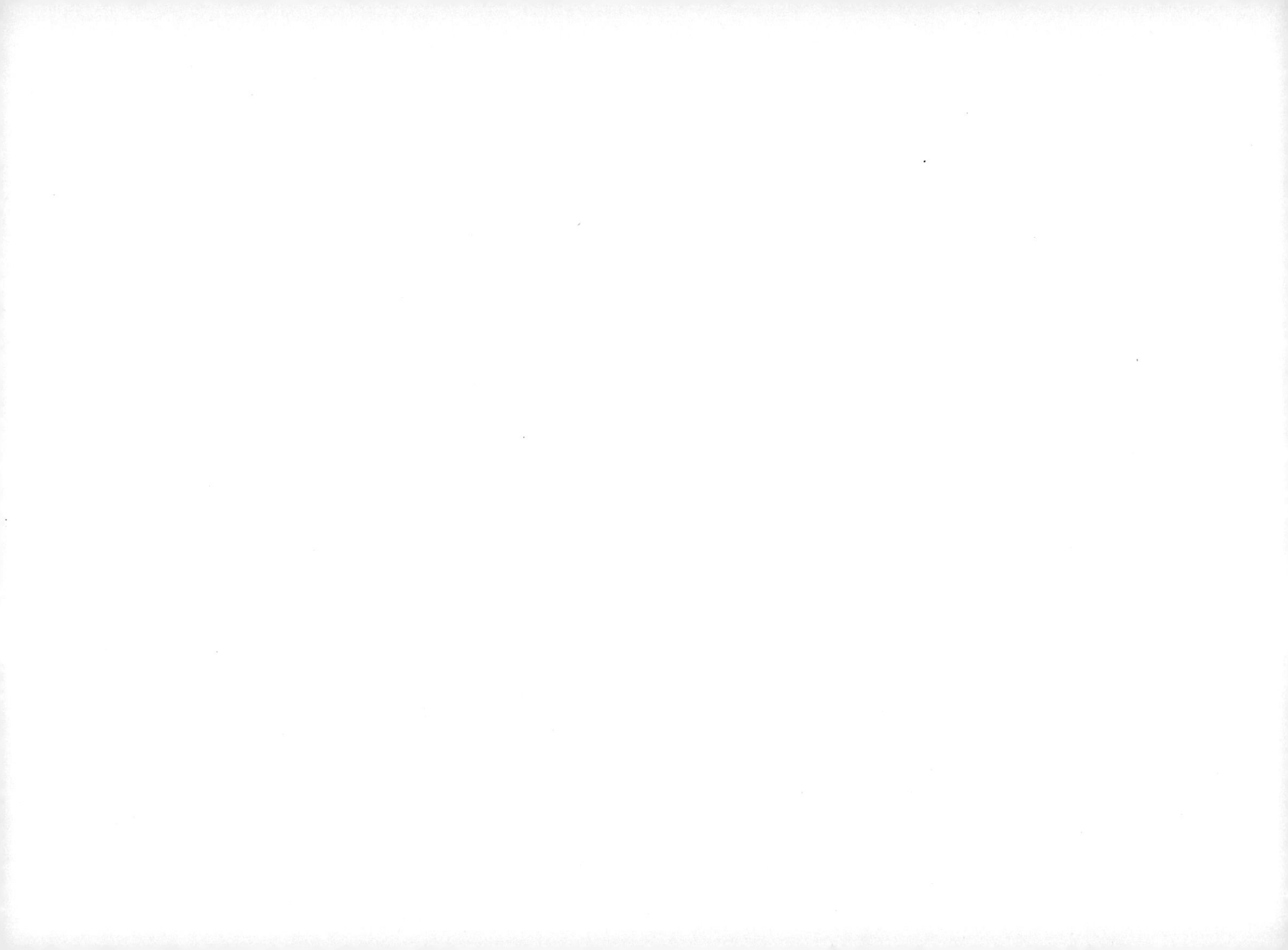

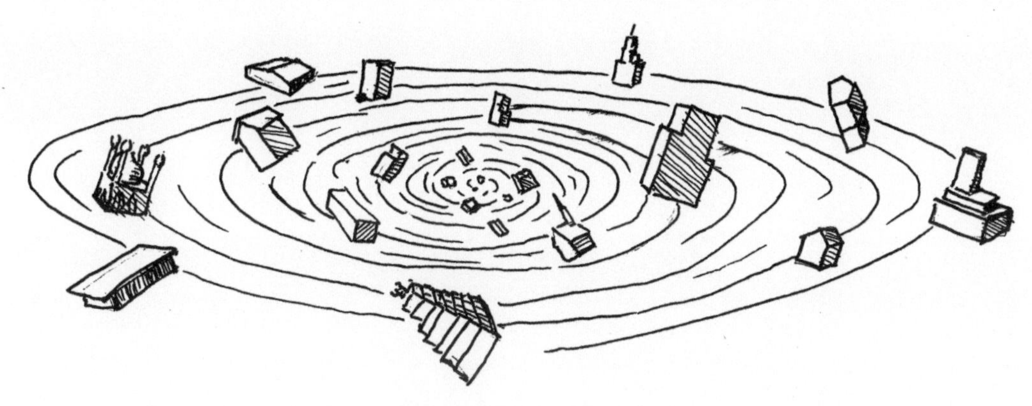

EDIFICE GALAXY

PART SIX

CAREFUL WHAT YOU WISH FOR

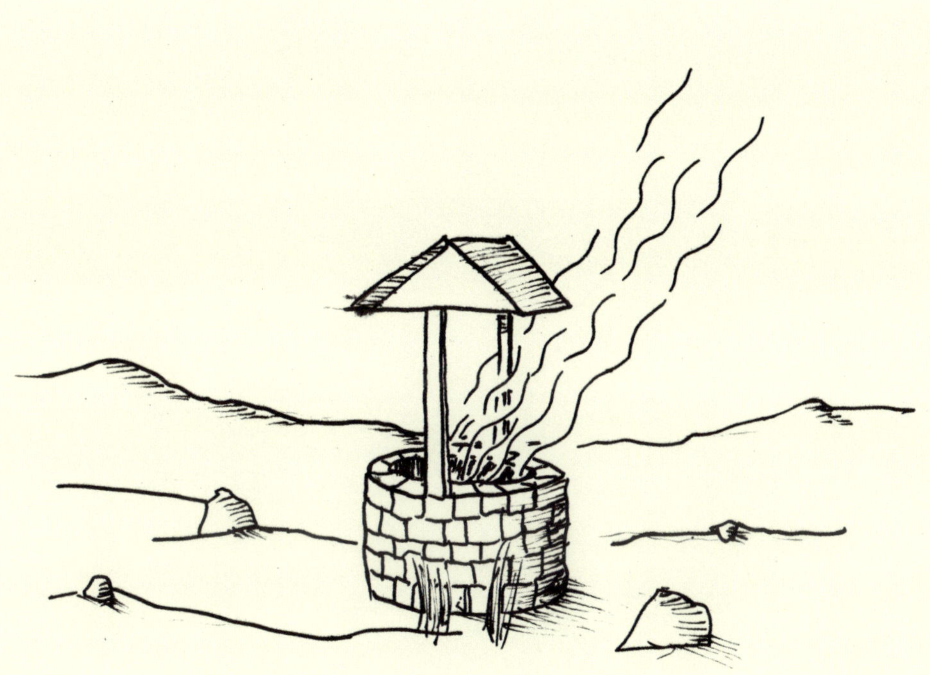

Don't look too much!
Don't stare too long!
The sweetness of the Devil's Candy.
The tender trap, the handsome hedonist.

Come here. But not too close!

Where are we going?

This is not what I expected.
Maybe I wasn't clear enough?

The magician gives the man a wish,
one wish.
That everything he touches turns to gold.
And when his wife and children are turned into statues
he retreats into the forest, never to be seen again.
Legend has it he starved to death.

Magic is real.
Dreams come true.

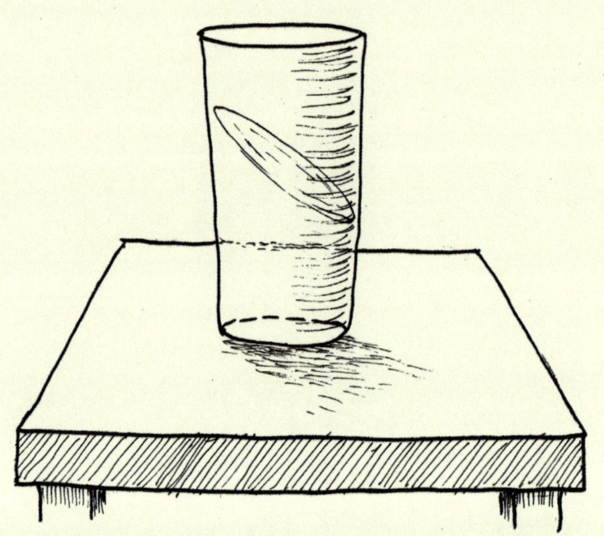

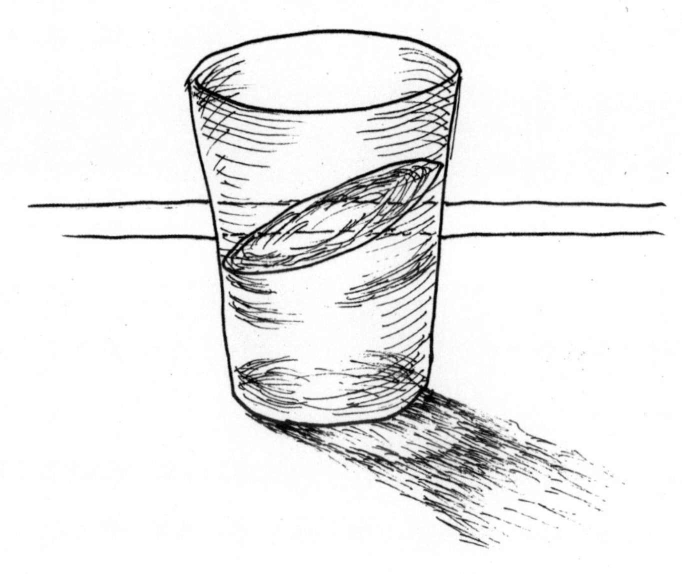

SHADY BUSINESS

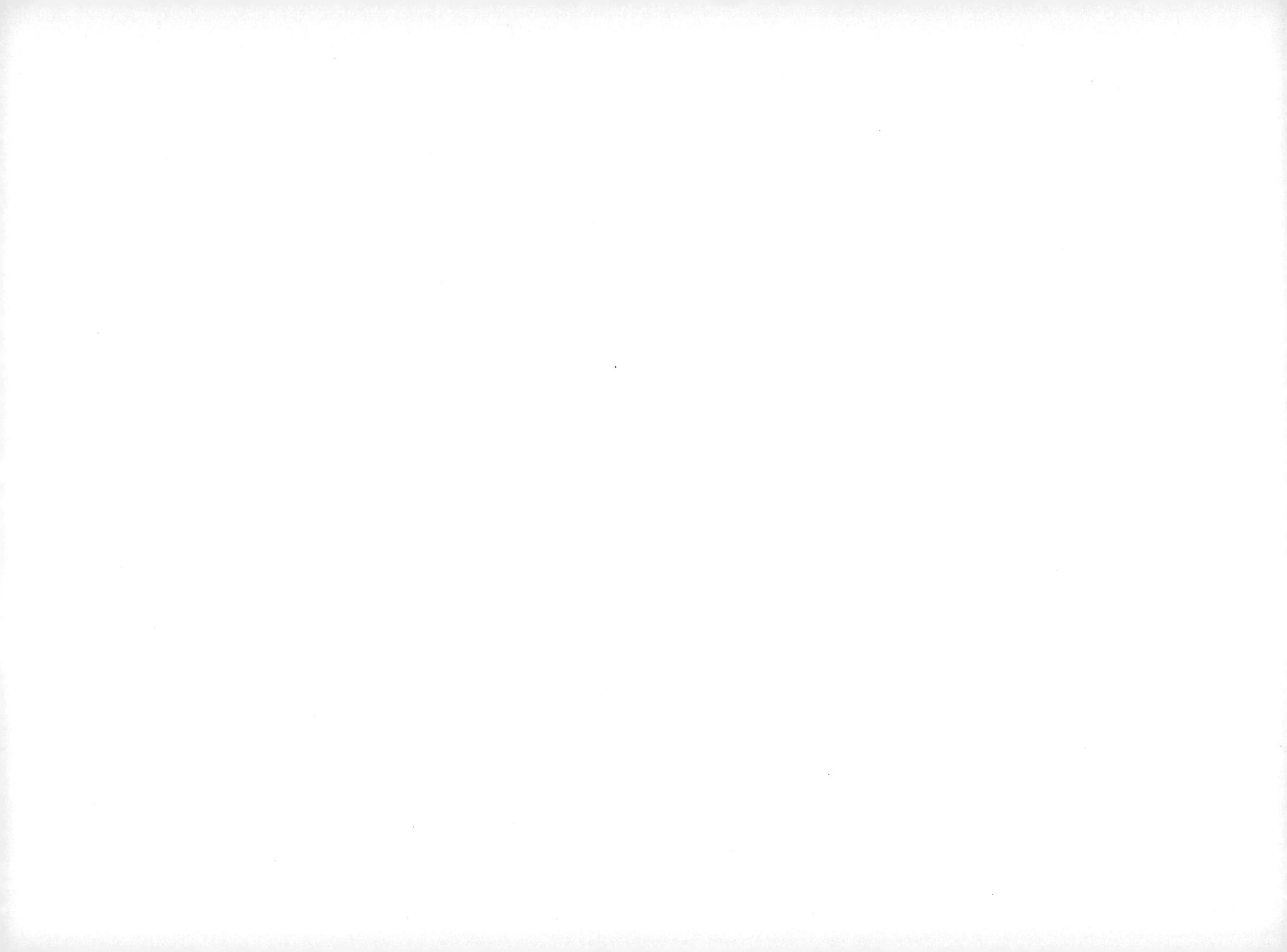

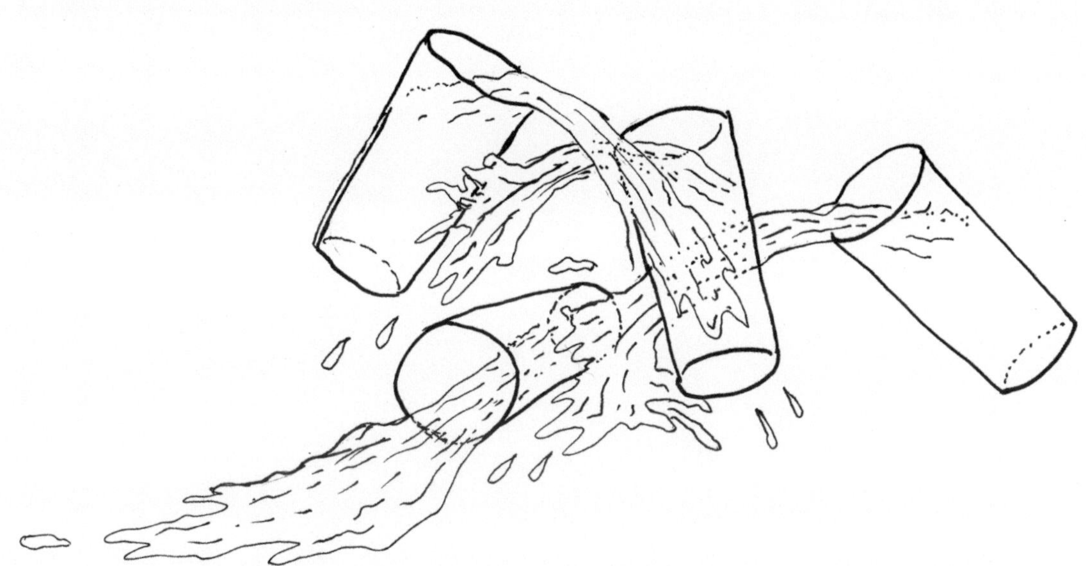

DON'T CRY

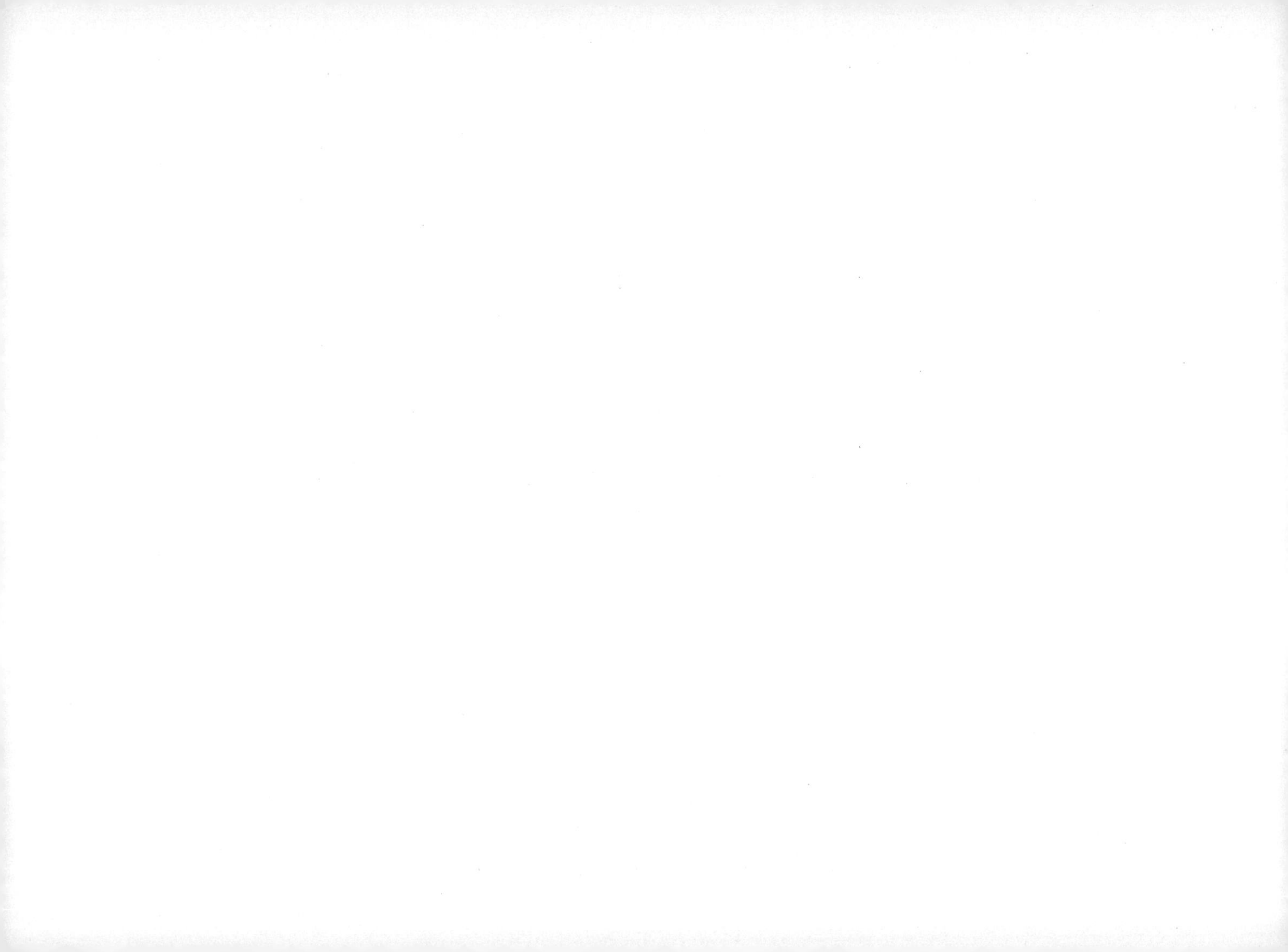

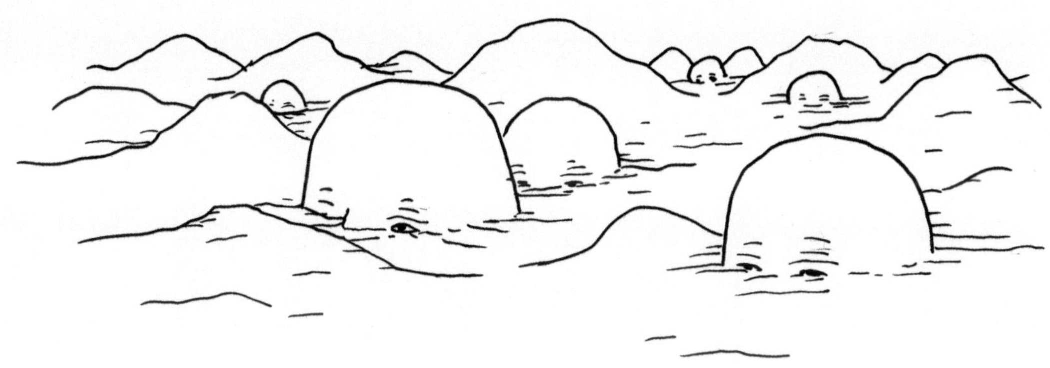

RISING TIDE DROWNS All BOATS

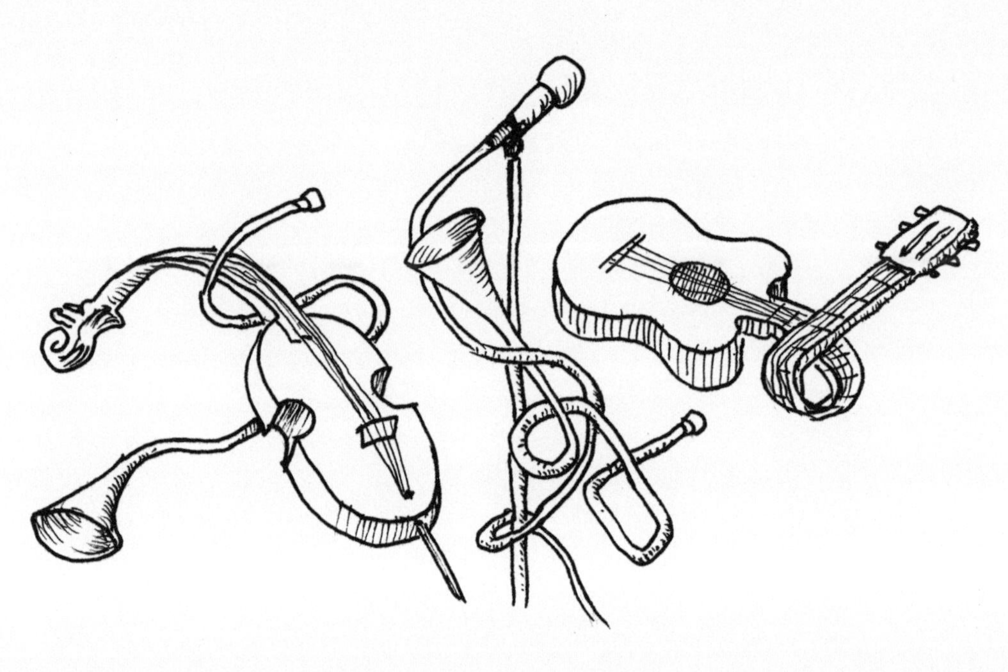

UNPLAYABLE MUSIC

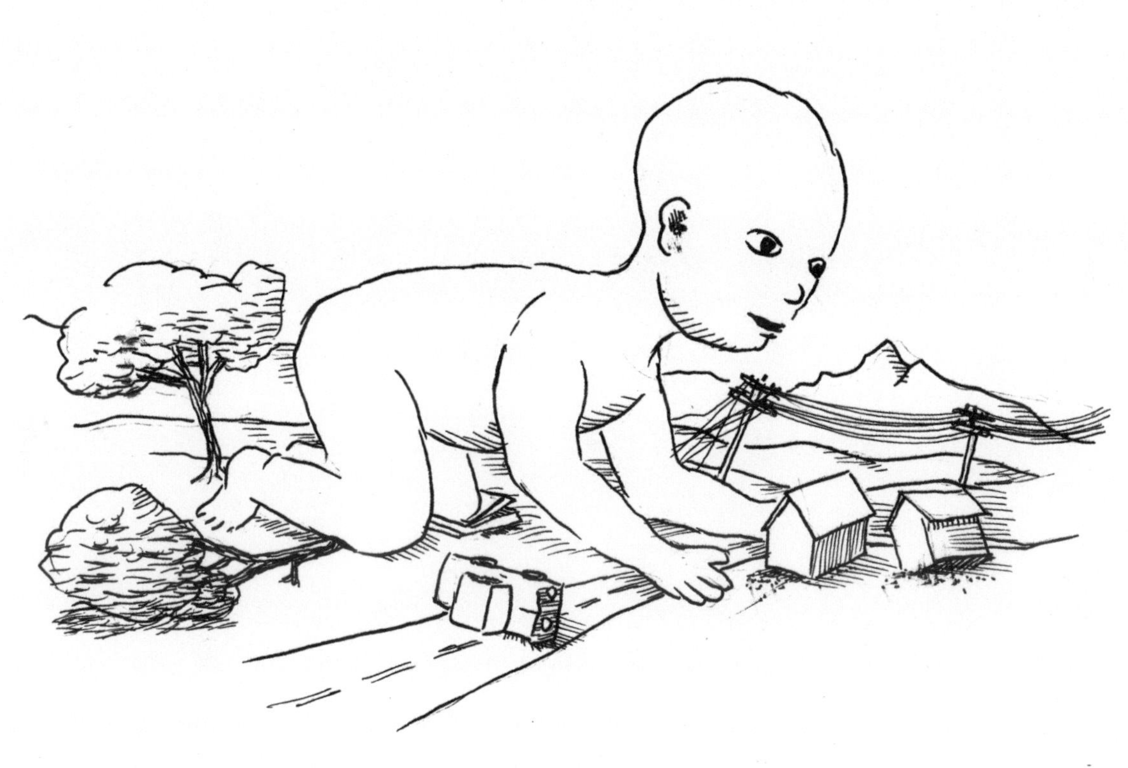

THE BIG BABY

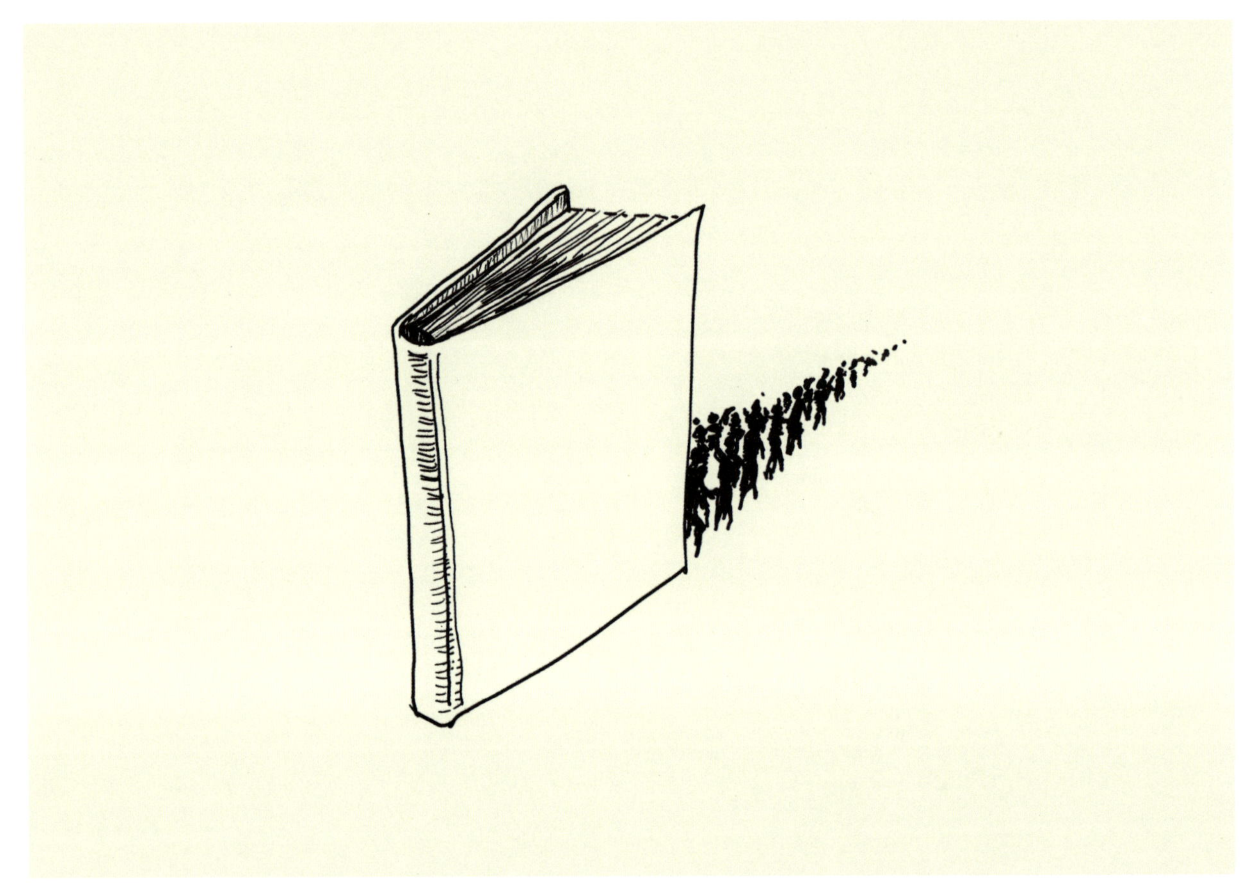

ABANDONING THE BOOK

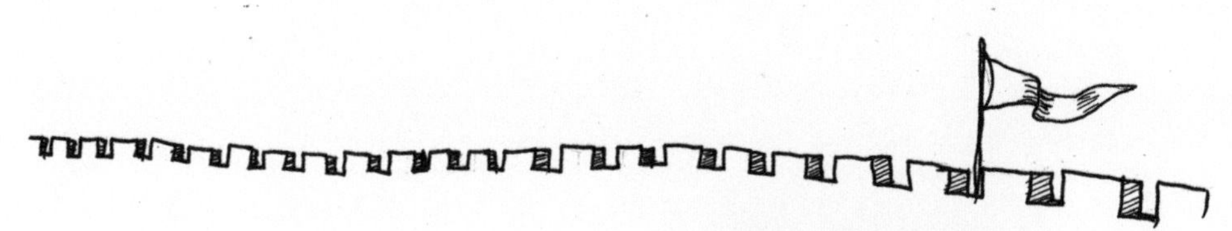

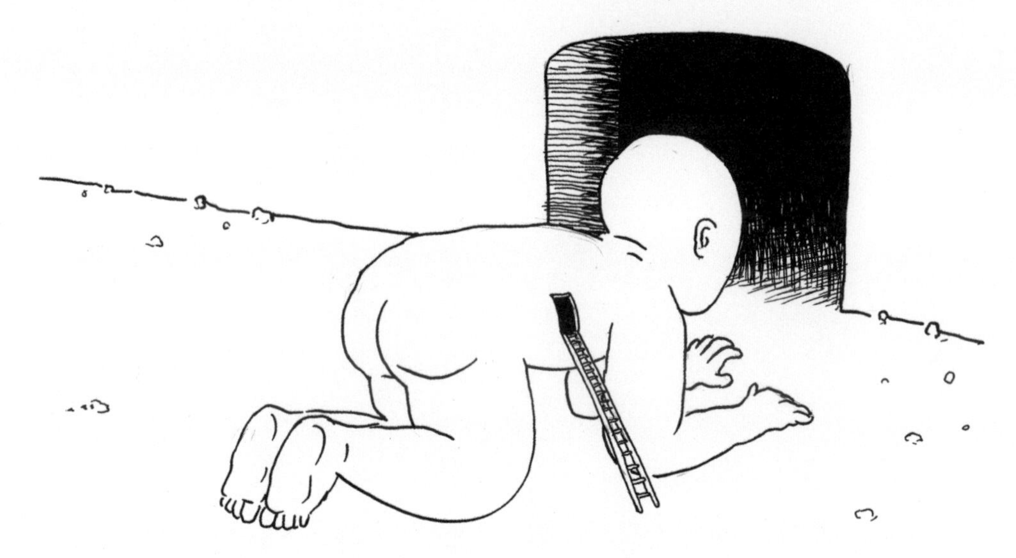

TROJAN BABY

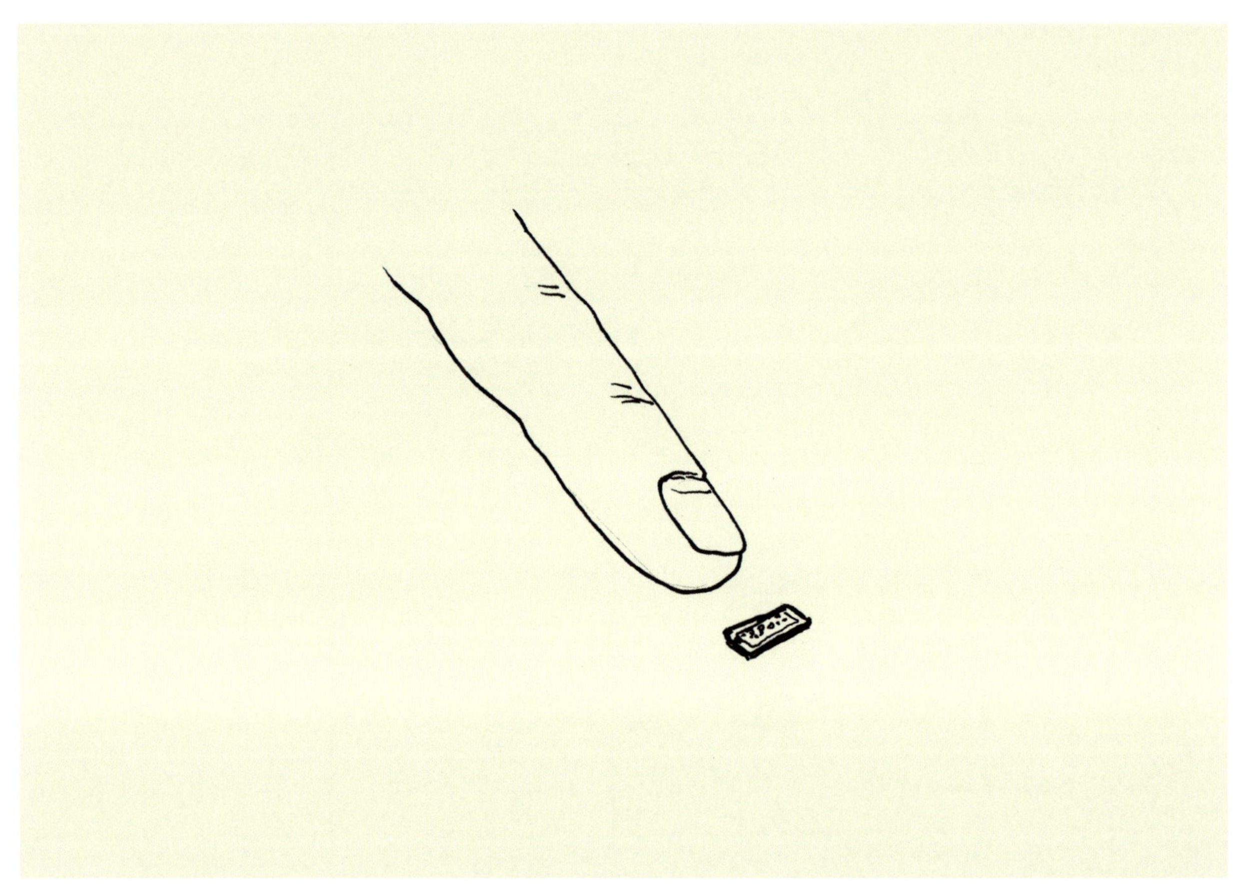

HYPER MINIATURIZATION

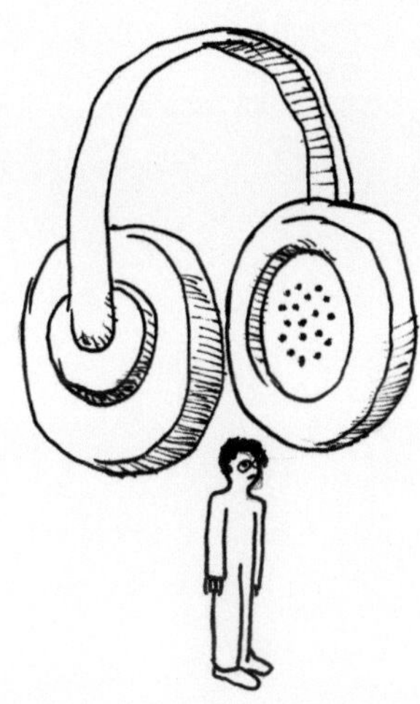

IMMERSIVE

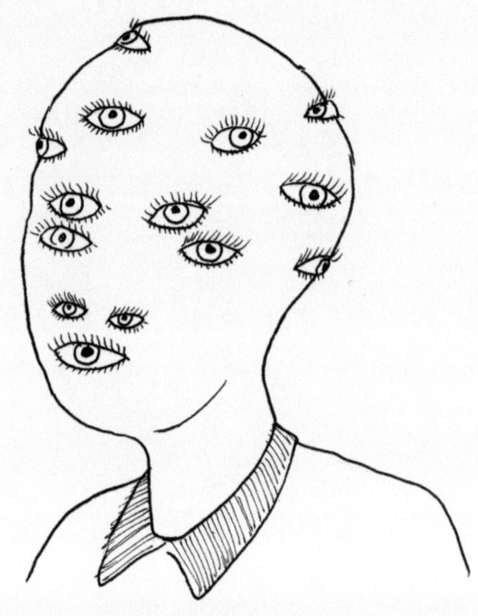

Ms. INTERNET

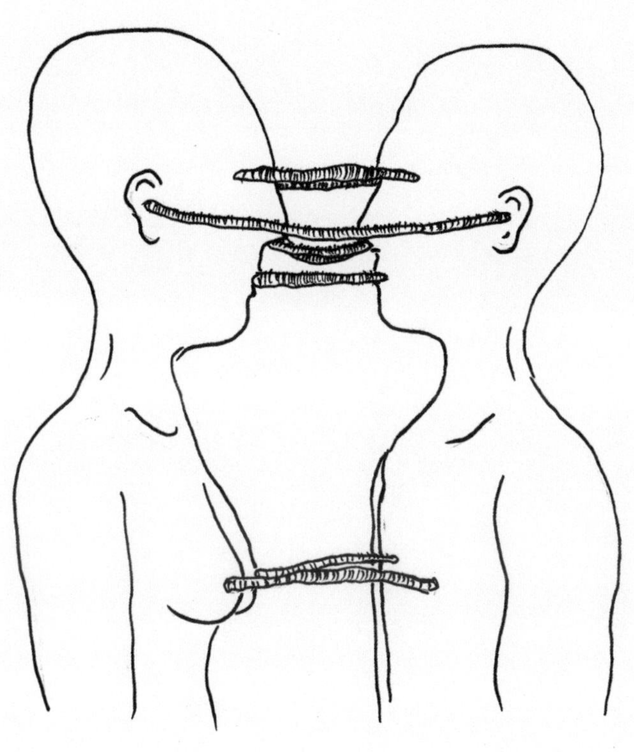

HOW WE DO IT NOW

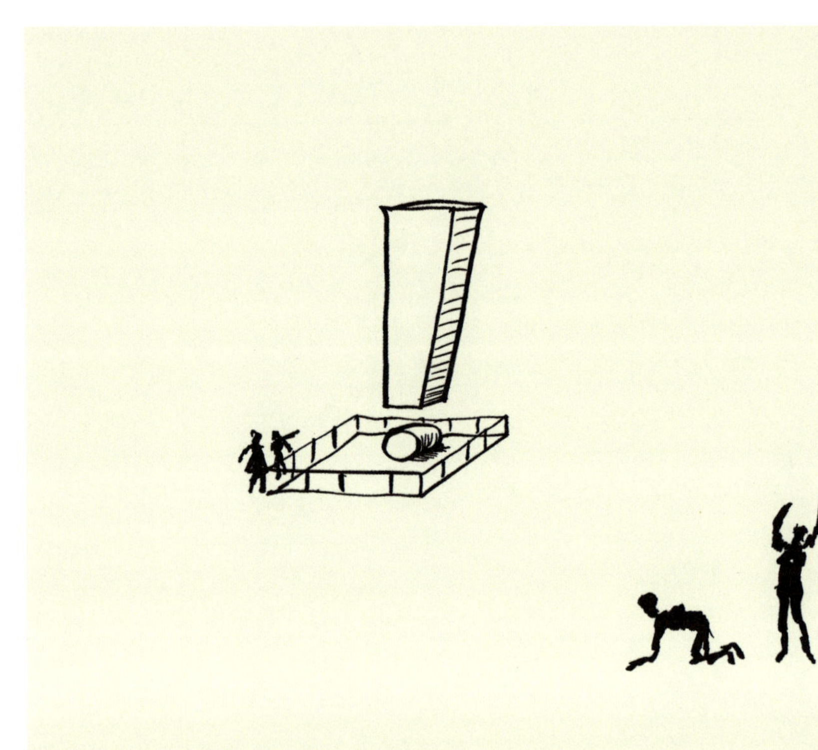

EXCLAIMING AT THE EXCLAMATION

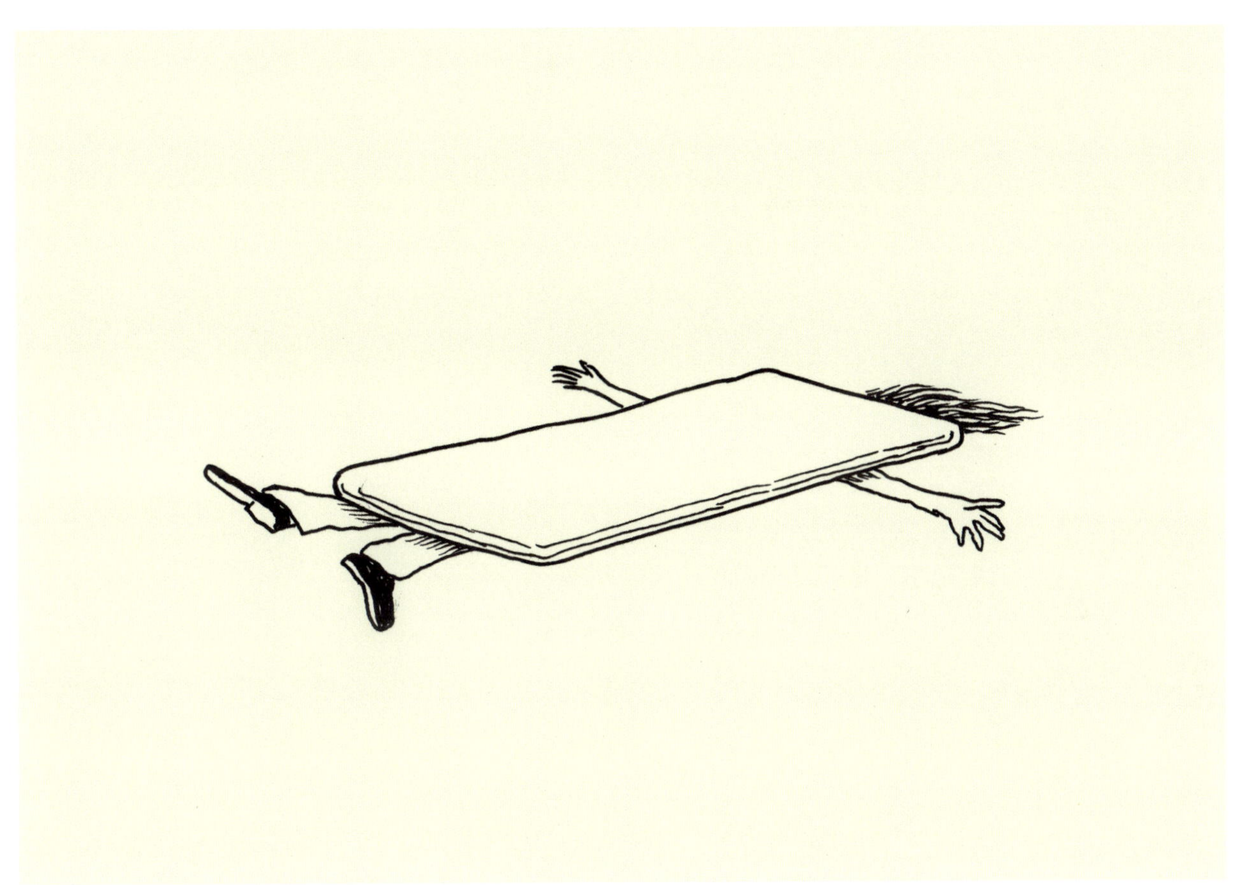

T.M.I.

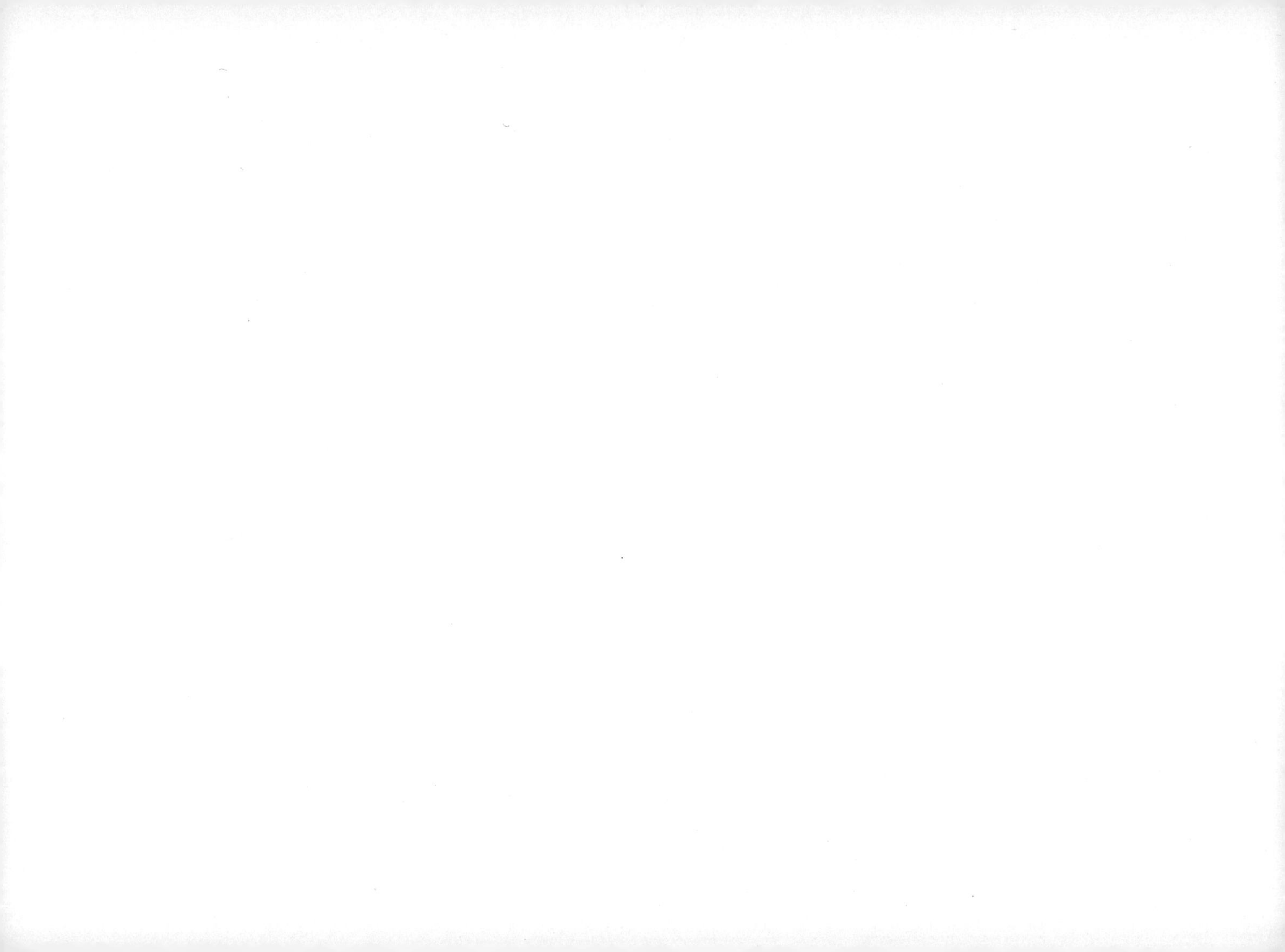

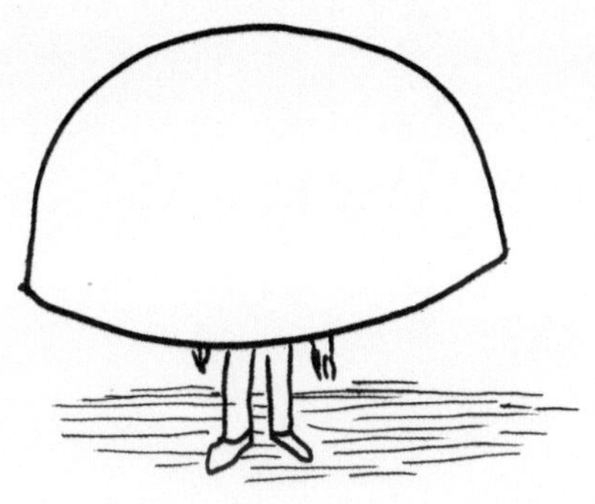

UNDER THE DOME

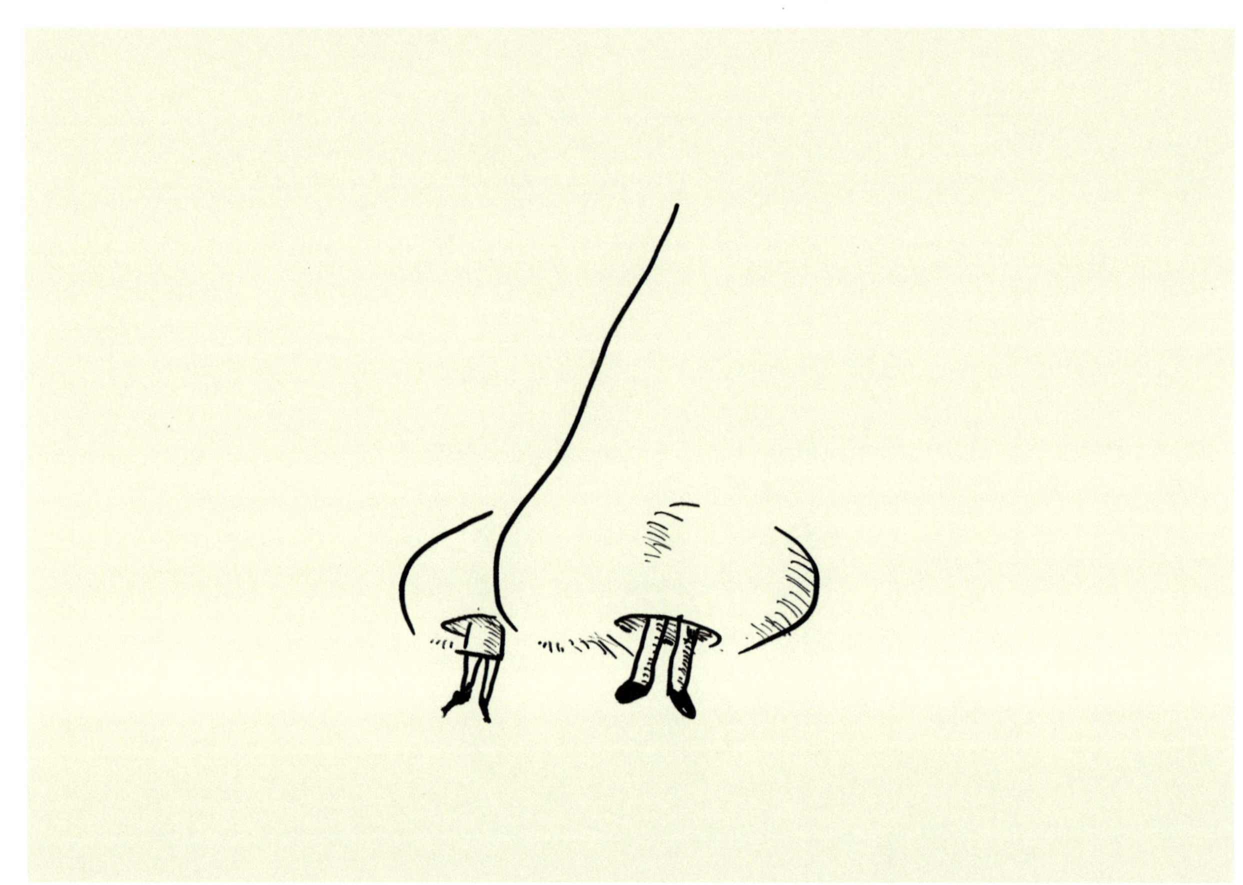

COVID EXAM

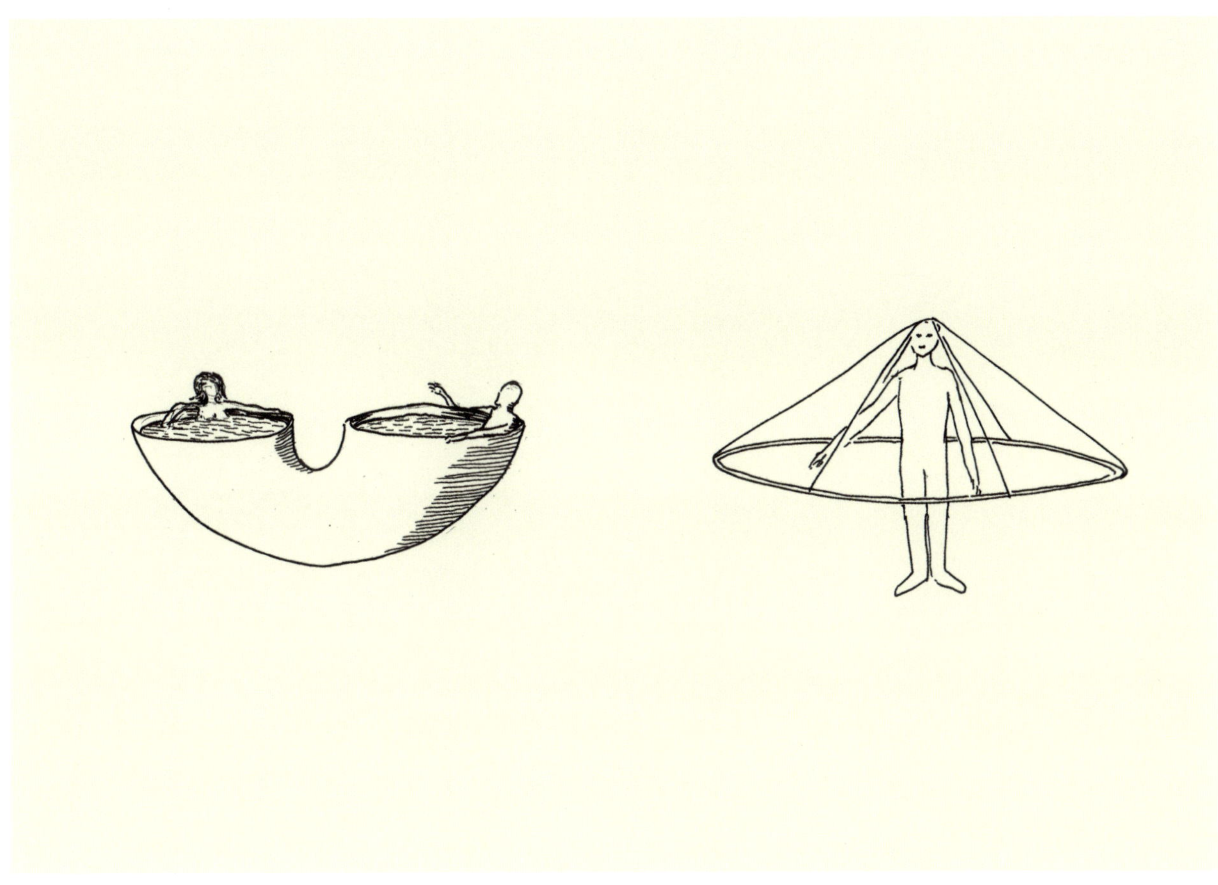

SOCIALLY DISTANT

SOCIAL DISTANCING HOOP

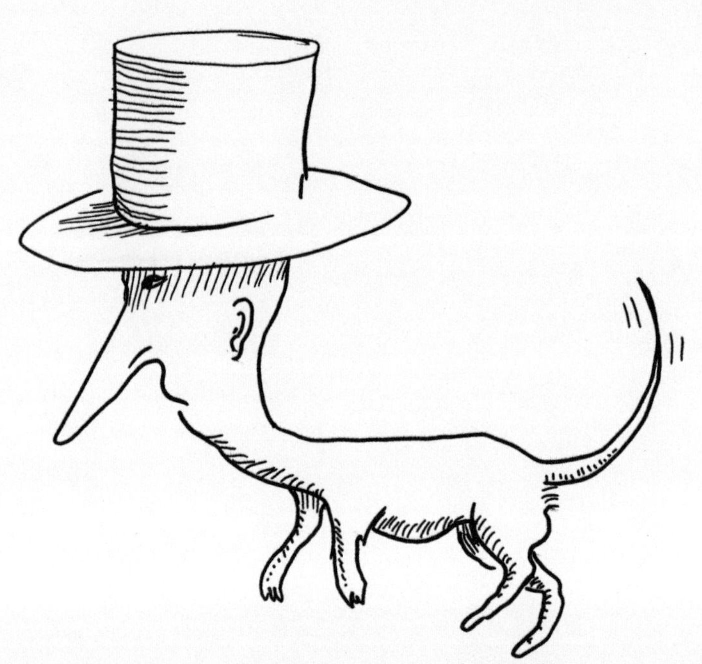

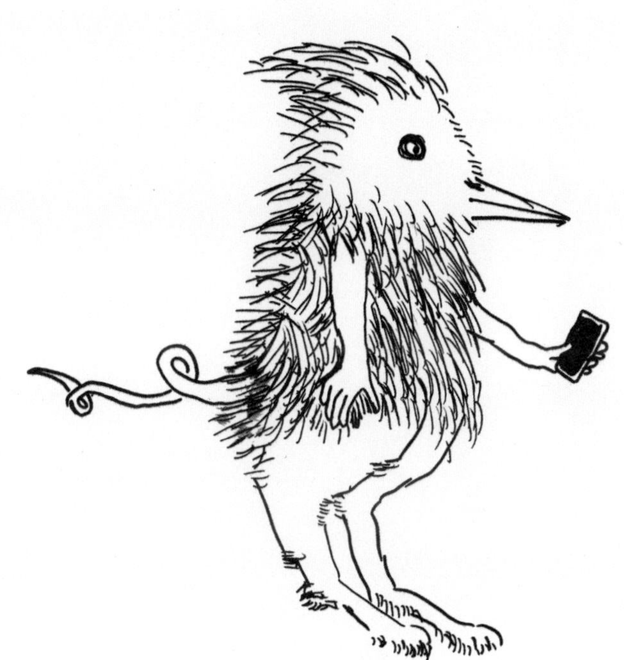

EPILOGUE

I watched every stand-up comedy streaming show for a year. Everything. I watched their performances on a laptop, connected to a Bluetooth speaker. (I couldn't watch dramas; we were living in one. Likewise, anything scary—are you kidding?) I watched all of it, there they were, live in person, somewhere, once upon a time. Sometimes I laughed, other times I thought, "This person is talking to the old world.
We don't live there anymore."

In the new world the rules have changed—
or at least there is the possibility of change.

The dogma of economic austerity has been left behind.
A society that exists for all of us is imagined as a real possibility.
Streets are for people. Everyone is out promenading.

The way things were, the way we made things,
it turns out, none of it was inevitable—
none of it is the way things have to be.
We can be different.

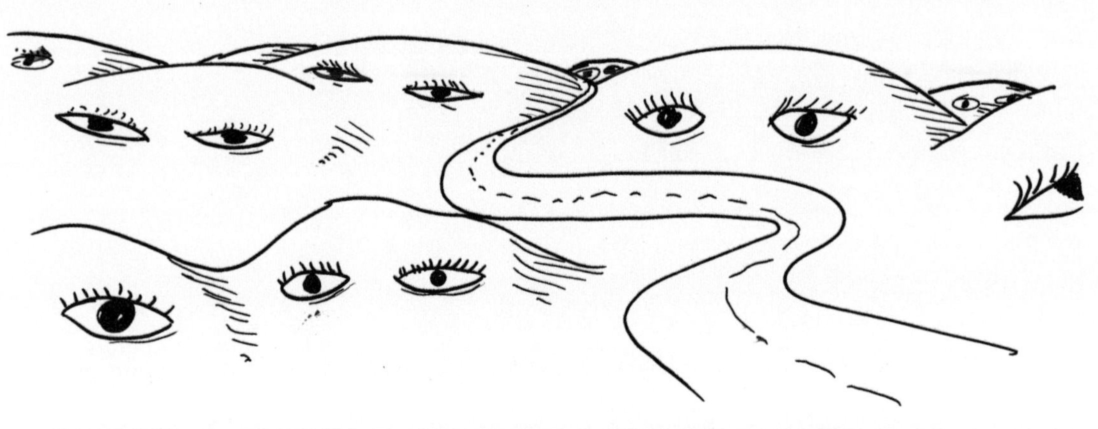

THE EARTH IS WATCHING

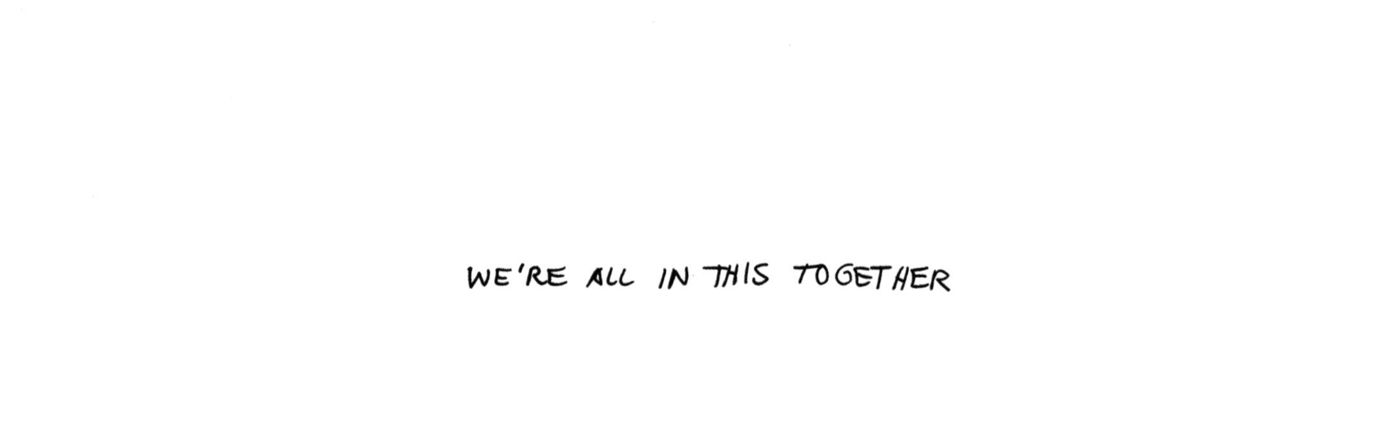
WE'RE ALL IN THIS TOGETHER

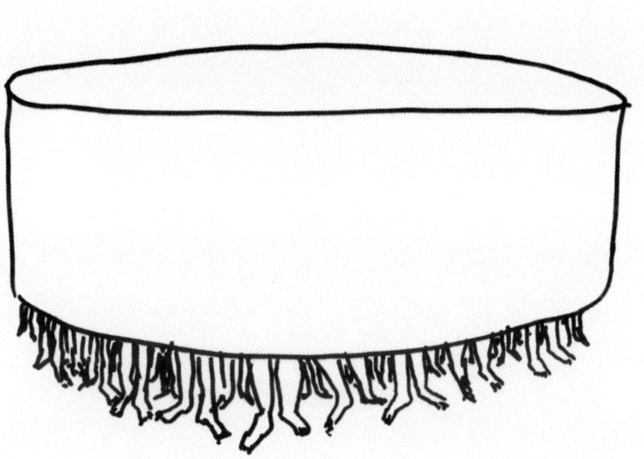

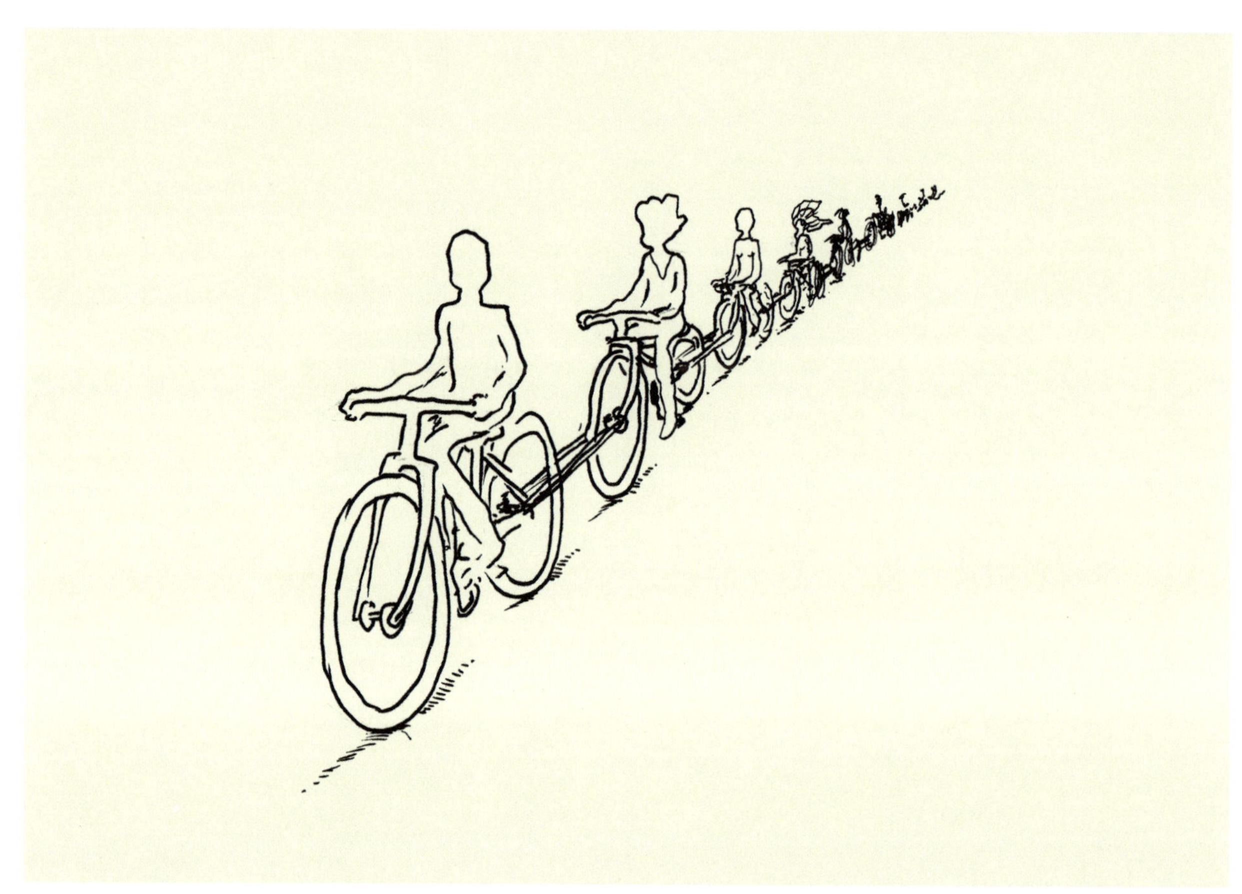

NO U-TURN

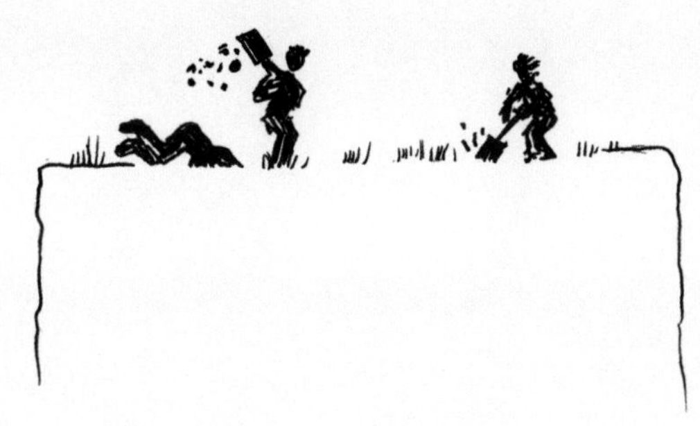

DIG DEEPER

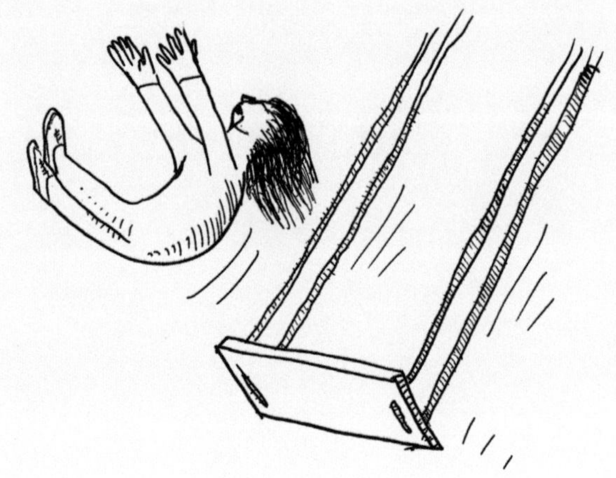

LETTING GO

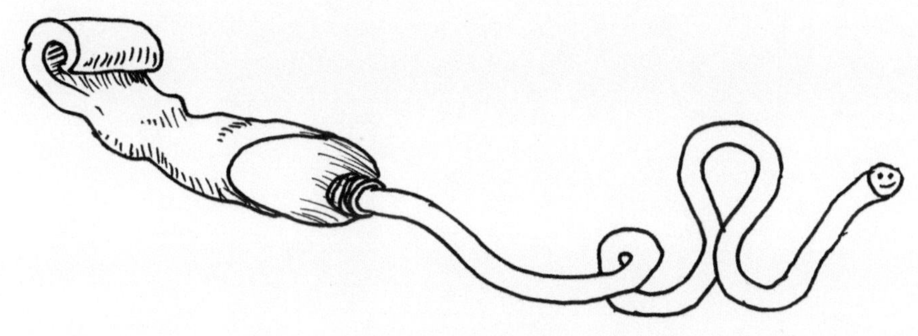

LIBERATION

IN A DREAM

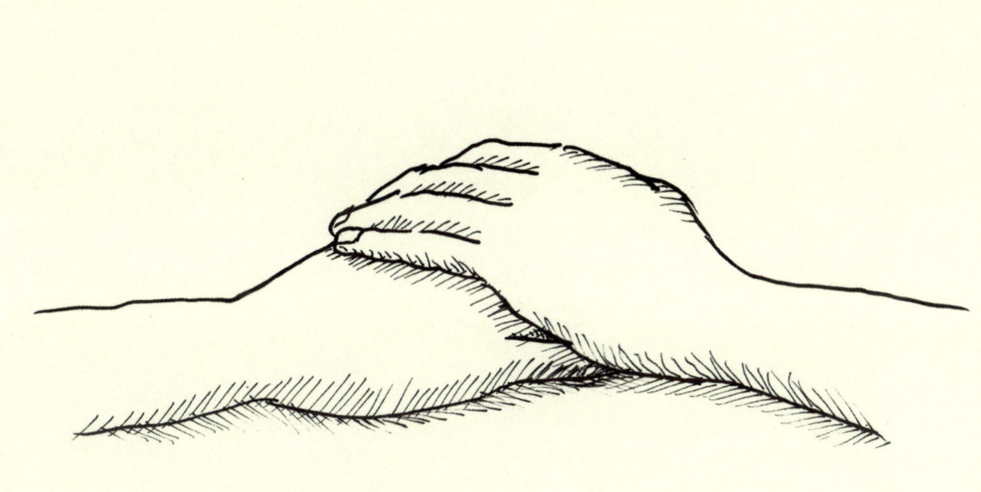

I AM MULTITUDES

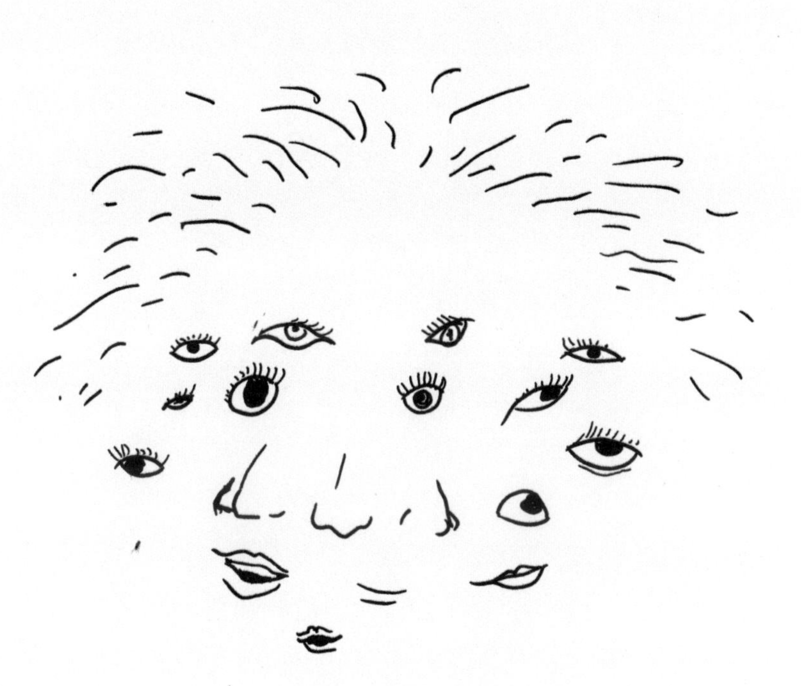

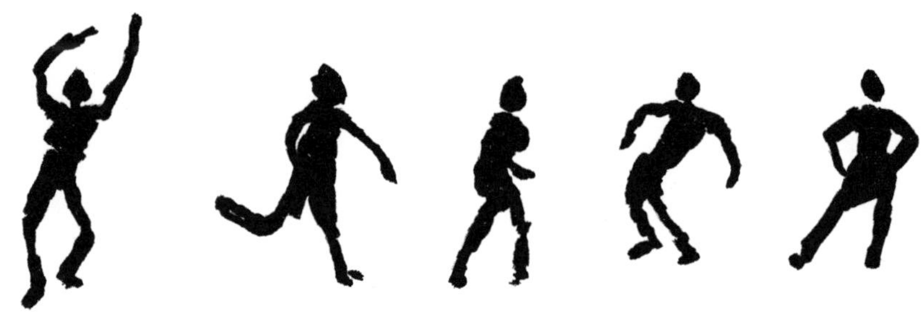

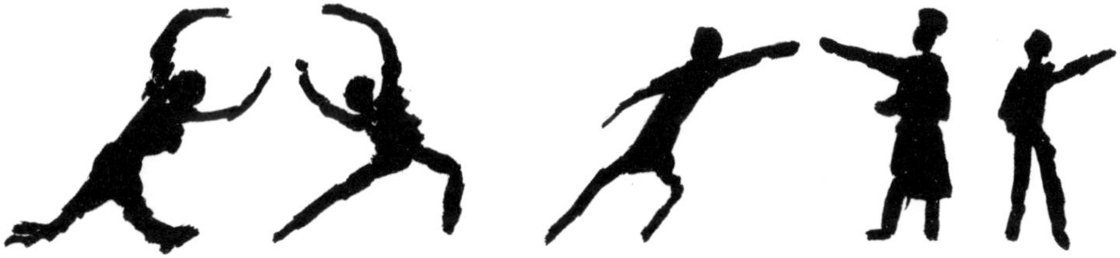

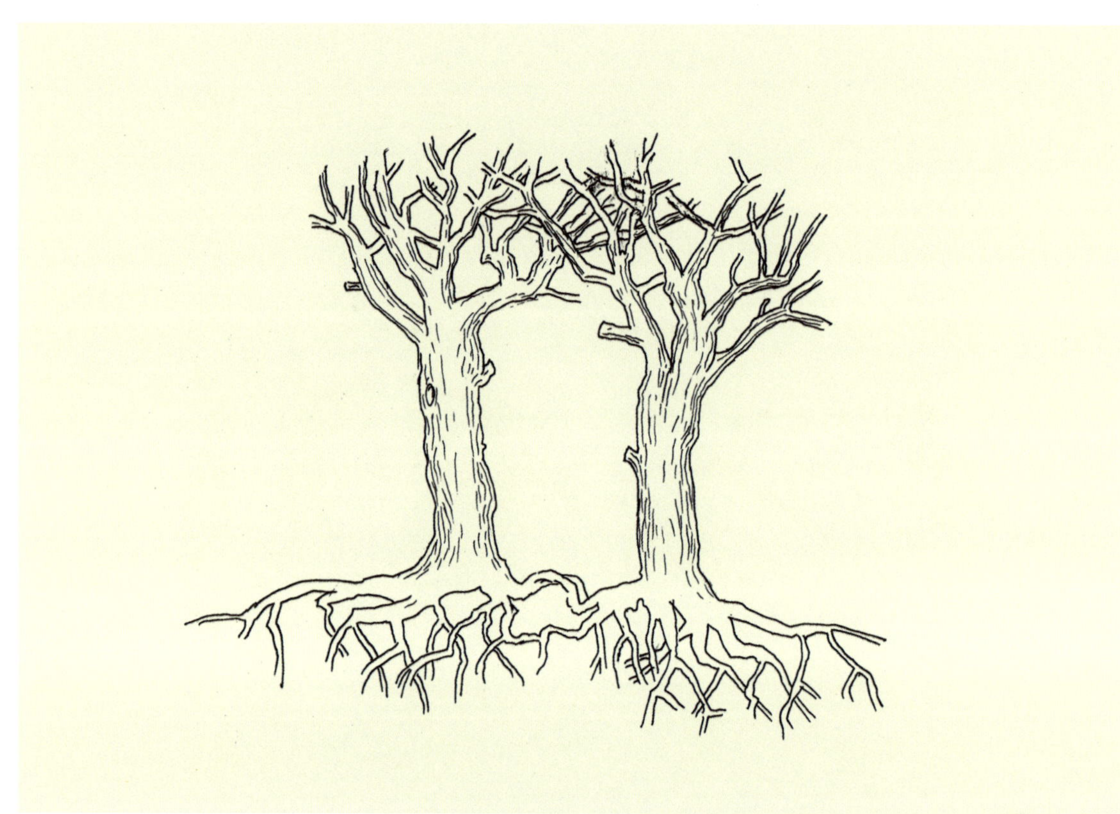

PALS

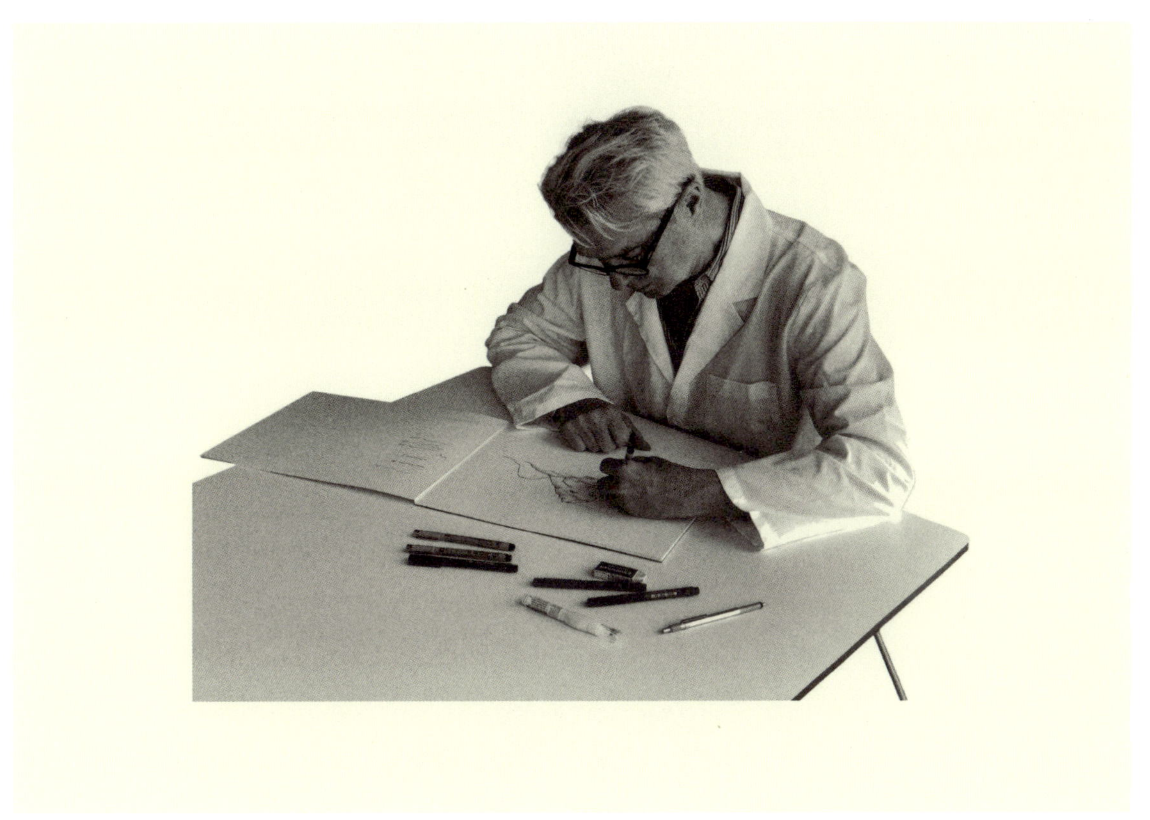

David Byrne, like many people, enjoys drawing.

David thanks Alex Kalman; Lauren Panzo and Marc Glimcher at Pace Gallery; Christine McLaren and Will Doig at *Reasons To Be Cheerful*; Mala Gaonkar; Karen Wong; Keith Fox and Deb Aaronson at Phaidon; Jin Auh at Wylie Agency.

Alex thanks David Byrne; Charlotte Sheedy; Jin Auh; Ian Keliher; Maia Murphy; Nerissa Dominguez Vales; Alex Eaton; Maira Kalman; Bruno.

Phaidon Press Limited
2 Cooperage Yard
London E15 2QR

Phaidon Press Inc.
65 Bleecker Street
New York, NY 10012

phaidon.com

First published 2022

ISBN 978 1 83866 511 1 (trade edition)
ISBN 978 1 83866 513 5 (signed edition)
ISBN 978 1 83866 512 8 (limited edition)

A CIP catalogue record for this book is available from the British Library and the Library of Congress.

Drawings and Words: David Byrne
Direction, Design, and Photography: Alex Kalman
Commissioning Editor: Deborah Aaronson
Project Editor: Maia Murphy
Production Controller: Nerissa Dominguez Vales

Printed in China